The Addario's Guide To Simplifying Home Safety and Comfort

BY Steven J. Addario

READ THIS BOOK TODAY IF YOU WANT...

- **... a home that is safe for your family**. Eliminate worries about the air you are breathing or the impurities you might be drinking.
- **... a home that is more secure for your family**. Stop worrying about the security of your family in the case of power failures, power surges, or even trespassers.
- **... a home that is comfortable for your family**. If some family members are too hot and others too cold, or if you have allergy sufferers in your home, you can make sure everyone feels comfortable and welcome at your home.
- **... a home that is even more beautiful**. Enjoy a gorgeous home that feels like a treasured oasis. Whether it's a simple thing like matching receptacles or an upgraded light or fan, or something bigger like a whole new bathroom, you'll find out more here.
- **... a home that is eco-friendly**. Learn the ins and outs of getting an eco-friendly home and reduce your environmental footprint without sacrificing quality.
- **... a home that is more convenient**. Discover the amazing power of home automation to make your life a little bit easier.

DEDICATION

This book is dedicated to everyone in my life that I have encountered over the last 40 years. You have all played a major part in creating the man that stands before you today.

To my Mom and Dad, Betty and Big Steve. I will never be able to fully express how grateful I am in words. Thank you for all that you have done. You have given me skills and talents that no one could ever take away and that will be worth more than any money, property or any trust fund anyone could leave someone. I hope I am making you proud. Love you both!

To my sister Nichole and brothers Joseph and David. You have always been some of my biggest supporters along this journey. I will always be here for you, your Spouses and my nephews and nieces. I commit to forging a way for our family's legacy to make its mark so our family name will never be forgotten. To my valued clients. Thank you for allowing me and my team of Experts to serve you.

To my wife, Alison. It seems like just yesterday we met in high school, now look at us twenty plus years later. We have been there for each other and through all of what life has thrown at us. I knew the first time we met that you would be my wife someday. Four kids, two dogs, chickens, guinea pigs and who knows what's next? You are my rock! Love your Lobstah

For my children, Steven, Isabella, Ayla, and Dante. I'm changing the world for you, and I'm empowering you to change the world too. Don't ever become stopped! You are and will always be more powerful than you could ever imagine.

CONTENTS

HOW TO KEEP YOUR HOME SAFE AND COMFORTABLE
FOR YOUR FAMILY

ACKNOWLEDGMENTS

I'd like to start by thanking my family, who support and encourage me to give my very best as I inspire my team to serve our clients daily.

I'd like to thank my team, who step up daily and represent Addario's Services as experts delivering their very best to Massachusetts families.

And of course I'd like to thank YOU, my valued client. You are my inspiration and the reason that my team and I show up and give our very best, every single day. Your family's safety, health, and comfort is our focus, and it's our privilege to serve you.

Thank you from the bottom of my heart,
Steven J. Addario Jr.

FOREWORD BY MIKE AGUGLIARO

Everywhere you turn, it seems like there's a new home services business promising "good customer service" when they deliver services like Heating, Ventilation, and Air Conditioning (HVAC), electrical, plumbing, drain clearing and more.

But when they show up to your home? Well, it's a different story. And a scary one.

... Maybe their van doesn't look great; maybe their tech has a messy uniform (if he's wearing a uniform at all); maybe their prices are high; maybe their level for customer service is low. And maybe you wonder if there is ANY trustworthy home service company that "walks the talk" and truly puts its customers first.

That's the unfortunate reality of the majority of home service businesses out there right now.

But I can tell you that there is one shining difference who stands head-and-shoulders above the rest, and that is Steven J. Addario and his company, Addario's Services.

When I think of high quality customer service in Massachusetts, there is only one company I think of: Addario's Services.

Hi, my name is Mike Agugliaro. Twenty-three years ago I founded and built the top-rated home service business in New Jersey, and I staffed it with experts. We recognized the same problem you do— that customer service is a rare thing among home service businesses—so we focused on providing the best customer service. Our customers loved it and we ended up serving tens of thousands of customers in the state, for which we enjoyed some state-wide and national fame.

I don't say that to impress you. Rather, I tell you that to explain how it was that Steven and I came to meet...

You see, I was growing my business in New Jersey; he was growing his business in Massachusetts. My business was a few years "older" than Addario's Services and we were being recognized throughout the state for our industry-defining customer service. We were being featured in newspapers, magazines, and on television.

And, because of the ground we were breaking in customer service, and the attention we were earning because of it, Steven reached out to me and asked me one question: "Mike," he said, "my company strives to provide the very best customer service in the state but I want to truly WOW them. Tell me what I can do to serve them at an even higher level."

I knew from that phone call that Steven and I would get along great, and I was more than happy to share some of my customer service "secrets" with him.

We ended up meeting regularly over a few years to discuss topics like how to lead the industry in service and innovation; how to hire the best experts in HVAC, electrical, plumbing, drain clearing, and more; and, of course, how to deliver the highest level of customer service in his state. (In fact, we still meet regularly today.)

From the moment we met, I was impressed with Steven's pursuit of excellence and his dedication for his customers. Sure, his outward appearance can seem tough and almost intimidating to someone who has never met him, but once he smiles and you get to know him you'll agree that he is one of the most down-to-earth people you'll ever meet, and someone who genuinely loves serving his customers.

I've had the privilege of meeting MANY home service business owners from around the world, and I can honestly say that there are only a few home service providers IN THE WORLD who are as dedicated to delivering the highest quality customer service as Steven. He is a world-class leader of a world-class company.

I'm proud to call Steven my friend and fellow "brother" in the home services industry. And, if I lived in Massachusetts, Addario's Services phone number would be in my phone's speed-dial as the ONLY home service company I would call to make sure my family was as safe and comfortable as possible in our home.

You hold in your hands a book that proves just how much Steven loves his customers: he put this book together to make sure that YOU are equipped with the very best information to make a great home-related decision for the comfort and safety of your family. It is filled to the brim with really solid, practical information that any homeowner would find valuable. (There's a reason that Steven has been featured on CBS, ABC, NBC, and Fox… it's because he's a knowledgeable expert who cares for his customers!)

If I were you, I'd read this book twice and make it a point to review this book every year to see if there are other ways to make my home an even better place for my family.

I'm proud to call Steven. my friend and fellow "brother" in the home service industry. And if you're in Massachusetts, I can't think of anyone better to serve you and your family.

Enjoy Steven's book… and enjoy a safer and more comfortable home for your family with the help of Addario's Services.

Have a better than great day,
Mike Agugliaro

PS, make sure Addario's Services phone number is on your speed-dial!
877-ADDARIO
(2 3 3 2 7 4 6)

DISCLAIMER

If you have a medical question, you go to a doctor. If your car breaks down, you take it to a mechanic. It's not likely that you would turn to a book to give you all the answers to your specific situation.

Likewise, this book is not intended to replace the analysis and recommendations of a home service expert, like those at Addario's Services.

This book is intended to be an introduction to the systems in your home, an inspiration to help you have a safer and more comfortable home, a troubleshooting guide, and a tool to help you make better decisions.

You should always consult an expert to improve your body, your car, and your home.

INTRODUCTION

Your home is your castle. After a long day at work, there's nothing like returning home to your family—to relax with them around the dinner table and to recharge with your loved ones.

The highlight of my day is spending time with my family at home, and I'm sure that's the same with you. The last thing you want to do is have to worry about whether your home is safe or comfortable.

You want your home to be safe and comfortable for your family. When it's not, you want to make it safe and comfortable again as soon as possible.

That's why I've dedicated my life to helping local families just like mine and yours to enjoy a safer and more comfortable home.

Hi, my name is Steven Addario Jr. and I am the founder of Addario's Services.

I've built a team of trusted experts who can help you no matter what the situation...

- Is the temperature too hot, too cold or inconsistent?
- Does your faucet drip?
- Do your lights, fans and receptacles work as they're supposed to?
- Are you doing a renovation and need to move pipes, wires or ducts?
- Are your drains clogged/backed up?
- Has the season changed and you need an HVAC system check-up?
- Is your home dusty?
- Are you concerned about water quality?

HOW TO KEEP YOUR HOME SAFE AND COMFORTABLE FOR YOUR FAMILY

These and many other situations that you may face in your home are the very things that inspired me to start my company, Addario's Services.

We've been in business for nearly 20 years. Along the way we've been able to help thousands of customers around the state, earning us an A+ rating with the Better Business Bureau, local and national recognized awards as well as being featured on ABC, CBS, NBC and FOX.

Perhaps you've driven past our building or seen our trucks on the road. Perhaps you've seen our company featured on local news stations or read my articles in the local paper. Maybe you've read my articles in the popular online site HomeownersNewswire.com, or you've visited our website, Addarios.com to get timely news home items.

We do all of this to serve you. Our team of local experts are available 24 hours a day, 7 days a week, 365 days of the year to provide you with the services you need, when you need them, to make sure your family is as safe and comfortable as possible.

Why do we do it? It's simple. We live in the area too. We're neighbors and friends. Maybe our kids go to the same school. We understand exactly how important it is that you keep your home safe and comfortable for your family.

We hear feedback all the time from homeowners who love the service we provide. For example,

...Bobby M. writes, *"Great service. Arrived on time when we needed. Well-mannered and very knowledgeable. . Reasonable price given the quality. Trustworthy and safety: would feel safe leaving the plumbers in my home if my wife or I were unable to stay."*

... Timothy D. writes, *"I had a great experience with Addario's! The team replaced my water heater. They were professional, courteous, and competent. They came out right away and the work was done efficiently. The installation looks very professional, which was important to me even though the water heater is hidden away in our basement. We upgraded to a tank-less heater and I noticed the savings in my gas bill right away. I highly recommend Addario's!!"*

...Chris G. writes, *"I have used Addario's a number of times for services such as a tank-less water heater, a new furnace, a new heat pump, thermostat and also some plumbing work for my outdoor sprinklers. Overall, I have found this company very responsive, extremely knowledgeable and professional in everything they do. Their products and service is top notch and they utilize great technology in their business practices. With this company, you are paying for quality and expertise."*

That's another reason why I wrote this book. Because I want to equip you with the ideas, strategies, tools, and decision-making criteria to help you enjoy your home and get the most out of it. And I hope to wow you like we've wowed the people I quoted above and thousands of others just like them.

So, whether you need an entire new HVAC system, or your home just needs some tweaks to make it safer and more comfortable, or if you want one of our experts to visit your home and make some recommendations, we are ready to serve you!

If we can help you in ANY way, please don't hesitate to reach out. You can find my company's contact information in the back of this book.

Steven J. Addario Jr.
Owner, Addario's Services Company

WHAT WE VALUE

I thought you should see this first.

It's important...

At Addario's Services, we have a set of Core Values that we believe in. They guide our decisions and actions every single day. I want to show these to you so that you know what we value. If you value similar things and want a company that relies on Core Values like these to guide them then we might be a good fit to work with you to make your home safer and more comfortable for your family.

Core Values—Overview

We raise the bar in everything we do: every team member, every action, every word, every service, every time. We actively seek opportunities to be better in this moment than we ever were before. When we each seek to raise the bar with these core values, we become unstoppable. – Steven and Joseph Addario

Core Value #1.—Safety First For Our Family and Theirs.
Think Twice, Act once
There's nothing more important than people. The safety of our team members and our clients will be valued above all else. There is never a good reason to do something unsafely. In every situation we will actively seek out ways to reduce risks, and we will always choose the safest way possible.

Core Value #2.—Deliver WOW Through Service
Exceed every client's expectations
Everyone serves: we serve other team members; we serve our clients; we serve our vendors; we serve the general public. So, every moment of every day we will check ourselves to make sure we are serving at the highest level possible. Our greatest reward is the feeling we get when we've served someone.

Core Value #3.—Highest Level of Integrity
Doing the right thing even when no one is looking
Truth. Trust. Reputation. Credibility. Integrity is essential because our reputation remains, long after we've finished a conversation or a project. When we work to enhance our reputation, we serve the team and clients by creating a predictably trustworthy experience. Honesty and "doing the right thing" are our golden standards.

Core Value #4.—A Great Place to Work
All for one and one for all
We are a team of individuals but we act as one. A single drop of water has little power but an ocean of water has immense power. Therefore, we honor and serve each other by working as one—working together, supporting each other, and standing shoulder-to-shoulder. When we work as a team, we are strong, focused, and unstoppable.

Why do we do what we do? It's all encapsulated in our one Core Purpose:

Core Purpose—To Help All People Live in Greater Safety and Comfort
We have a noble calling at Addario's Services. We enrich the lives of local families by making sure they are safe and comfortable. There is no higher purpose in life. We view it not as a job but as the highest privilege to be entrusted with this responsibility. We take it seriously; we pursue it relentlessly, and we serve tirelessly.

Here's what our trucks look like…

And when we show up for an appointment at your home, our team members will pull up to your house in a vehicle like this… and they'll always be wearing a clean, crisp uniform and a name tag, so you'll always know that it's one of our experts.

Look for our trucks in your neighborhood—we're serving your neighbors too, to help keep their home safe and comfortable for their family!

PART 1.

READ THIS SECTION FIRST… (YOU MIGHT BE VERY SURPRISED AND IT COULD SAVE YOU A LOT OF MONEY!)

You invest in your home. And the return on that investment? It's more than money. It's safety and comfort. And when it comes to your family, you're probably willing to spend whatever is necessary to keep your family safe and comfortable. But wouldn't it be nice if you could save a bit of money along the way? Find out how by reading Part 1 of this book.

HERE ARE 8 REASONS WHY YOU SHOULD READ THIS BOOK RIGHT NOW

This book was written for YOU. It was meant to help and empower you. And it was given to you by someone who cares about you and your family. Here are 8 reasons why you should read this book right now.

1. **Ensure the safety of your loved ones**. Sure, you might define your family in different ways (we like to say that family includes the people we are closest to) but the bottom line is: they are your family. You want to do everything you can to keep your loved ones safe. This book will clearly lay out the best ideas, information, resources, and strategies to help you keep your family safe.

2. **Enjoy a comfortable home**. Once you have the confidence that your family is safe, you also want to make sure they are comfortable. Home is an oasis from the busy world, and this book will help you create a home that is welcoming and comfortable.

3. **Protect your home**. Your home is probably one of the biggest investments you've ever made (it is for most people) so of course you want to make sure that you protect it. A single, good decision could extend the life of your home for years to come. (That not only helps to ensure your home remains intact but also ensures your family's safety and comfort, too!)

4. **Increase your home's value**. Since your home is one of the biggest investments you've ever made, wouldn't it be nice if you could increase the value of that investment so it was worth even more if you ever decide to sell? Although there are many factors outside of our control that can influence the selling price of a house, we know that taking care of your

21

home's systems, including installing systems that buyers love (such as a modern high-efficiency furnace or a water filtration system) can potentially help to increase the value of your home relative to others in the market.

5. **Make faster, better, more confident decisions**. You are busy! Between work, your social life, and the kids' soccer practice and your volunteer activities, you don't have a lot of time in the day for other things. So, if you ever need to make a decision about your home—such as if you need a plumbing repair or to invest in a new air conditioning unit, it can be a daunting task to try and squeeze that into your schedule, especially since these are systems that most people don't have a lot of familiarity with. This book is written to give you an overview of the systems in your house, figure out how best to take action, and also help you make better, more confident decisions about what steps to take.

6. **More time**. You plug in a desk lamp and turn it on. Nothing happens. What should you do? Many people aren't sure. So you try a few things or call a family member or friend who might know. This book is written to help you instantly get the answer and take action to figure out what's wrong.

7. **Save money**. If something happens in your home, you may not be sure how to fix it, which means you might try to fix it yourself or you may hire someone else who is not qualified to fix it. Ultimately, this costs you more money than if you hred an expert fix it right the first time. Reading the information in this book will help you to know exactly what to do, and that will help you save money by making the right decision with the right expert.

8. **Less stress**. You already have enough to deal with in a day, you don't need another thing to occupy your mind! This book will help you figure out the best decisions quickly and confidently so you can skip the stressful decision-making and get back to living the life you want to live.

HOW TO KEEP YOUR HOME SAFE AND COMFORTABLE
FOR YOUR FAMILY

We've written this book to serve you and your loved ones. Take the time to read it so you can create a safe, comfortable, beautiful home!

HOW TO USE THIS BOOK TO MAKE YOUR HOME SAFER AND MORE COMFORTABLE

This book was written for people who own and care for homes. If you have a home in your care, and want it to be safer, more enjoyable, and even more valuable, then this book is for you.

- Homeowners
- Landlords and property managers
- People caring for other family members
- Those who have inherited a home
- Those who own a second home (such as a rental property, cottage, or shore-house)
- Even renters who want to make sure that their rental unit is as safe as possible, and who want to be better informed about home buying
- Real estate professionals who want to understand the inner workings of houses that they are helping people buy or sell

It doesn't matter whether you live in the home or simply care for it on behalf of someone else. If you want to know about a home and want to care for it better, keep its occupants safe, and even increase its value, then we have written this book specifically for you. Throughout the book we may use the word "homeowner" but what we really mean is YOU—the person who owns, uses, and cares for the home and its occupants.

This book is non-technical, which means that you don't need any experience in the systems described—like your home's HVAC system, the plumbing system, the electrical system, etc. This book will give you everything you need to know.

This book is not intended to replace expert advice from qualified, licensed, experienced professionals. Rather, this book is meant to help you understand what you, as a homeowner, should know to help you confidently interact with a professional.

Ultimately, this book is meant to give you confidence about your home and a clear game-plan to ensure your home is as safe, secure, comfortable, and valuable as it can be.

To help you, this book was written to be used in 3 specific ways:

1. You can read it from cover-to-cover in order to fully understand your home. We recommend you read this book cover-to-cover at least once, perhaps even more often than that, to get the big picture.
2. You should skim this book each year to build a game-plan to constantly improve your home.
3. You can use this book to dive into the specific sections you want to know more about. For example, if your air conditioner starts making a funny noise, simply turn to the air conditioner section of the book to learn more.

Reading this book as a whole gives you the big picture so you can feel more confident about your home; skimming through year after year helps you create a game-plan so you can make your home even more safe and beautiful; and diving in here or there when necessary empowers you with a tactical approach to care for your home.

There's one more way that this book will help you: it introduces you to me—the author—who is your ally when it comes to the care and safety of your home and family. So, please feel free to reach out to me (my name and contact information is listed in the back of the book) and I'll make sure that my team and I serve you at the highest level.

THIS WILL SURPRISE YOU...

Some people might look at this book and think it's about how to maintain and repair a house. But nothing is further from the truth. In fact, you might be surprised to discover what this book is really about...

According to a survey by the Department of Housing and Urban Development (HUD), there are approximately 125 million to 135 million houses or "housing units" in the United States. This number includes single, detached homes as well as apartment units and mobile homes.

That's a lot of *houses*. But only some would be called *homes*. There's a difference between houses and homes.

Many of those millions of houses stand empty. Some are short term rentals. Some are being built, while others are being torn down.

If you've lived in more than one house in your lifetime, you may have called each one home... for as long as you lived there. But once you moved away, it continued to be a house but was no longer your home.

There may be millions of houses but what makes a house YOUR home?

Most of us think of a house as a structure—there are walls, a roof; there are doors and windows.

But when you think of home, what do you think of? For most people, a home is more than a structure: a home is a retreat from the craziness of the world that you look forward to returning to at the end of each workday; a home is the smell of turkey at Thanksgiving and the sound of talking around the dinner table; a home is where you can take your shoes off, wear comfortable clothes, and put your feet up; a home is where you share laughter and warmth and love; a home is where you make memories with your family.

Sure, no home is perfect and you may not be able to relate to all of the elements we listed above but for most people a home is a place of refuge that's all their own, away from work and community, where you can typically feel comfortable and safe and be yourself around your family.

Family. Your family. There is nothing more important in life. That's what a home is all about. It's about being with your loved ones. —the definition of which may vary from one family to another, and may include parents and children, grandparents and grandchildren, adopted families, extended families, close friends, and even those furry four-legged family members too!

The definition of family has changed over the years but one thing hasn't changed: our commitment to YOUR family... whatever that looks like.

A wonderful family makes for a high-quality life. Like most people with a family, you would do anything for yours to ensure their safety, health, and comfort, and to build long-lasting memories with them.

I love family. I have my own family (and I think of my employees as family, too). Like you, my team and I do everything we can to ensure that our families are safe, comfortable, and happy. As home service providers, we've dedicated our lives to serving families in the local area to help them—YOUR family!—enjoy a safe, comfortable, beautiful, and happy home. This book is NOT really about home maintenance and repair; it's really about helping your family.

Every page has been written with YOUR family in mind. Every day our team of experts shows up at our headquarters and then goes out into the community to see how we can help and serve your family.

The building you live in is not just a house. It's your home. It's where your family makes memories. This book is really about helping your family enjoy a place to make memories for years to come.

HOW TO BENEFIT FROM THE BIGGEST FINANCIAL INVESTMENT OF YOUR LIFE

Your home. For most people, it's the biggest financial investment of their lives; perhaps it is for you as well. That's why most Americans save up for a down payment, acquire a mortgage loan to purchase their house, and then live in that investment for a few years. It's why we want to have a positive financial outcome if and when we choose to sell. It's why we invest in our homes to protect our investment and to even increase its value.

We protect our homes by maintaining the systems that keep our homes safe and comfortable. For example, we maintain the electrical system to ensure we get power whenever we turn on a light switch or plug something into the wall, and also to ensure that our homes are safe and protected from the threat of fire, which can happen with improper wiring.

We also try to increase the value of our homes by investing in maintenance and upgrades that will be potentially attractive to buyers if and when we choose to sell. One common example is an HVAC system. Home buyers are looking for homes that are easy to maintain and efficient, so if you get a high efficiency furnace and air conditioning system installed, you may attract buyers who are looking for a hands-free home.

These are the obvious financial reasons to invest in the care and maintenance of your home's systems.

There are more financial reasons to care for your home and invest in the maintenance of your home's systems...

We also protect our wallets by maintaining our home, too! A dripping faucet or an inefficient furnace costs money. Every drip that keeps you awake at night is a few cents down the drain. Day after day, those cents turn into dollars that appear on your water bill! Every time your inefficient furnace runs, it costs more per square foot of your home to heat, which appears on your heating bill!

And, should your water heater burst, or some other home system disaster occur, you're faced with an even heftier bill to repair, replace, and clean up.

What's more, maintaining your home also protects your financial situation in another surprising way: your health. From the water that your family drinks to the air that your family breathes, your homes plumbing, electrical, and HVAC systems work together to keep your family healthy. But if ignored and not maintained, your family could get sick from the impurities in the water or in the air. And the cost of the healthcare implications of a sick family member can be astronomical. A small, proactive investment now and then to maintain and upgrade your home can help to keep your family healthy for life.

There are yet other reasons why your home is the biggest investment of your life, and it may surprise you... It's far more than the biggest FINANCIAL investment. It's much deeper.

Your home is an investment into your family's safety—safety from natural disasters and other weather-related situations, safety from threats like fires, and safety from intruders. When people know they are safe, they are more confident, comfortable and happy, and are better able to thrive in the world. A home that protects you and your family delivers that sense of confidence and comfort.

Your home is an investment into your own mental health and sanity, providing you with a retreat from the busy world. That is a priceless reward of living in your home.

Your home is an investment into your time. A home that is not maintained and cared for can be costly and time-consuming to live in. Yet, maintaining your home proactively by using the strategies in this book will help you to enjoy a carefree home.

Your home is an investment into the future. When you provide a safe, comfortable, beautiful, happy home for your family, you are creating an environment where your children can grow up, and where your loved ones can thrive, by giving them a safe place to call their own. This allows them to go out into the world and be successful, because they have the confidence that they can return to a safe place to live. And if you have children, your home will be a model for them as they grow and have children of their own. Thus, a well-maintained home is a legacy that will last.

PART 2.

HOW TO ENJOY YOUR BEAUTIFUL HOME AND MAKE IT SAFER AND MORE COMFORTABLE FOR YOUR FAMILY

Your home is your castle. So, why would you ever want to settle for anything less than the best? In Part 2 of this book we'll look at how you can make your beautiful home even more amazing to live in. You won't believe how amazing it is to live in your home when you know this information. Just imagine how your family will feel, too, when they come home from work or school and enter a safe, comfortable, beautiful home that welcomes them. You'll learn how to do that in this part of the book...

YOUR AMERICAN DREAM

The American Dream. It's the lifestyle goal that has inspired millions of citizens since the foundation of our country.

Since the earliest days, the American Dream included the new-found ability to choose your own career instead of working at a career that your family or social level thrust upon you; it included your ability to ascend as high as you wanted financially; and it included your ability to own your own home.

Although we take it for granted now, home ownership is a an amazing privilege that brought some of America's earliest settlers here. They escaped the over-crowded cities of Europe where a home was something they'd have to rent for excessive sums. But here in America, a home was something available to everyone.

Today, the American Dream is as much about homeownership as it is about your ability to rise as high as you like on the financial or social ladder. The home you own is part of your own family's "stake" in the American Dream.

For most of us, a home is the single biggest purchase we'll ever make in our lives, which is why many people need a mortgage to be able to acquire a house.

There's a reason why so many of us willingly take on the debt and responsibility needed to acquire a house: Because your home is not just a structure, it's a statement that extends through history and proudly claims that you can choose your own path in life and you are building an amazing future for your family.

By extension, then, your home is really about your family. Your family sets out each day to go to work, go to school, and socialize, but you all return to your home as a place to be safe and secure from the world outside. No wonder people call their home, "their castle!"

Your home is not just a purchase, it's an investment. That's a critical concept with some surprising lessons for us: we understand what it means to invest financially (such as in the stock market). An investment should provide a financial return on investment.

Financial Returns. Chances are, you bought your home partially because it would do just that – you hope that the home you bought will rise in value during the time you live there so that it will be worth more by the time you sell it.

And what makes a home such a powerful financial investment (versus other financial investments) is your ability to control and direct the rise in value. A coat of paint throughout the house could add a few hundred dollars to the price of the house when you choose to sell it; a brand new bathroom could add a few thousand dollars to the price of your house when you choose to sell it.

But your home is more than a financial investment. Yes, you take care of your home because you hope for a financial gain when you sell but your home is far more than just the potential money you'll make.

Unlike other investments you'll make in your life, your home is an investment that delivers other kinds of returns...

Safety and Security. We live in a crazy world – and every time we turn on the news, it just seems to get even crazier. So our homes have become a safe haven – a safe port in the stormy world we live in.

When disaster strikes, or when a difficulty rears its ugly head, what's the first thing we do? We head home to be with our family and make sure they all safe. It's a natural instinct that is heightened by our home ownership.

No matter what struggles we face at work or on the commute there and back, we have the confidence that when we pull into our driveway, we're home. We're in a safe place where we can be ourselves and we're free from the onslaught of confusion and danger that runs rampant outside of our home.

So your home is an investment into your family's safety and security.

Health. A healthy family is a top priority for everyone. We know that the choices we make and the foods we eat and the exercises we do will all contribute to a long and healthy life. Likewise, our home is an investment into our family's health.

Maintaining our home actually contributes to a healthier family – from water quality to air quality, from waterproofing to wintertime heating – we can help improve the health of our family by making careful choices about our home.

So that's the next way that your home is an investment – by contributing to the health and long life of your family. You make your home healthier and the return that you get is improved health for your family.

Comfort. You work hard each day. So when you come home at night, it's critical that you have a place where you can relax and be comfortable. That's another way our homes provide value to us – they are a place where we can relax and unwind after our busy days.

If we didn't have a few moments of peace and quiet, could you imagine how much harder life would be? This downtime is absolutely necessary for us to be healthy and even to maintain our sanity!

So our homes are an investment into our comfort – into our ability to just put up our feet and spend a few minutes of calm in the storm of the world. We buy a home because we want the "return on investment" of some peace and quiet where we can recharge our batteries before going back out into the world.

Memories. Perhaps the most overlooked way that our homes are an investment is also perhaps the most important way – because our home is a place to build memories with our family.

Our home is a place where you'll spend time with your family to create wonderful memories. You'll look back and think fondly of times around the dining room table for Thanksgiving or curled up in front of the fireplace on a winter evening. Each passing day is an opportunity to build memories that you will cherish for years to come, when your family has changed and grown and perhaps your children have children of their own.

So your home is an investment into wonderful memories – and the "return" is the memories that you'll enjoy forever.

If you own a home, you own a piece of the American Dream. And, for many people, that piece of the American Dream is part of their financial nest egg that will protect and grow their family as well as their net worth.

Therefore, it only makes sense to build on that privilege and legacy by caring for that home—that American Dream investment—to expand the value you enjoy and the impact you can have.

This book will equip you with the ideas, resources, tools, and strategies—plus give you the confidence—to care for your home and keep it safe and comfortable for your family.

YOUR INVISIBLE HOME

When you invite someone to your house, you often give them a visual cue to help them find your house. "It's the house with the blue door," or, "It's the first house on the left after the park," or, "It's the house with the big oak tree in front."

Although you can SEE your house and can describe it, you are really only describing a small part of your house. The walls and roof make up the structure of the house. But there are many things happening inside your house that are invisible even to you, and these are the components of your home that contribute significantly to your family's safety and comfort.

These systems work 24/7 – whether you're aware of them or not – and they all contribute to your quality of life.

HVAC system. HVAC means, "Heating, Ventilation, and Air Conditioning," and it's the system that primarily controls the temperature and air flow in your house. Want your house to be warmer or cooler? Does your house seem stuffy, dusty or breezy? Your HVAC system controls that.

Electrical system. This is the system that powers your house. It runs your kitchen appliances so you can enjoy cold and hot food; it powers your clocks so you're on time, it powers your entertainment devices so you can watch TV or browse the internet. In most cases, your electrical system also connects to the municipal grid so you get power supplied from an outside source.

Plumbing system. This is the system that controls the flow of clean water coming into your house.

Drain/Sewer/Septic system. This is the system that takes unwanted wastewater out of your house. In towns and cities, plumbing systems typically connect to a city grid so that the water you bring into your house and send away are part of a larger urban plumbing system. In less populated areas, you may have a septic system to remove waste.

These are the systems that most people have in their homes. In nearly every home in America, there are HVAC, electrical, plumbing, and drain systems at work.

In addition to these systems, there are other systems that some people have for even greater safety and comfort—systems that sometimes connect to the systems above or systems mentioned that stand alone and these systems simply give you even more peace of mind as a homeowner. They include…

Waterproofing. There's another system that many people overlook – it's a system that keeps outside water outside your home. This includes your roof, your gutters, your landscaping, your weeping tiles, and other waterproofing around your house.

Indoor air quality. This system, most likely connected to your HVAC system, improves the air quality in your home. It removes allergens and other airborne impurities, allowing you and your family to breathe more clearly.

Water filtration. Water filtration and purification is another system that attaches to your home's existing plumbing system, providing you with cleaner, safer drinking water.

Home security and automation. Home security and automation provide a variety of tools to monitor the inside and outside of your home for trespassers, to lock and unlock your home without the need for keys, and even to automatically adjust your home's temperature from your mobile device!

Generators. These power your home when the electrical system is disrupted (e.g., when there's a storm that knocks the power out to the neighborhood).

Your house is a series of systems that work together.

It's similar to your car: your car is a series of systems that work together in a certain way to help you get where you need to go.

It's similar to your body, too: your body breathes, blood courses through your veins, your heart beats, the food you eat fuels you so that you can live.

Your house, your car, your body – these are all a series of systems that work together for a purpose.

In the case of your home, its purpose is a place where your family can be safe, healthy, comfortable, and build memories.

Take Care Of Your House

When your car stops working, you take it to a mechanic to fix.

When you don't feel so good, you visit a doctor who can help figure out what the problem is and fix you up.

You know you shouldn't wait until your car or body no longer work before you have an expert look at them. You know that preventive maintenance is a powerful investment to ensure that your car and your body work correctly at all times, and that any cause for concern is addressed as soon as possible before the problem becomes more costly in the future.

Your home is the same in many respects: you take care of it to keep all the systems working at their highest level of performance and you should use preventive maintenance to make sure you identify any potential problems before they become costly hazards and headaches.

Whether you're looking at preventive maintenance or a breakdown, you need to take it to an expert to fix. Ironically, your house might be the largest investment you've ever made, there isn't one certified specialist you need to call – often, there are experts for each system in your house. Only through regularly scheduled, proactive check-ups will you ensure that your house is as safe and comfortable as it could be for your family.

WAYS TO MAKE YOUR HOME SAFER

As we've said, a house becomes a home because of your family—whether your family includes children, extended family, friends, or the four-legged furry variety! And you'll do anything for your family to keep them safe.

This chapter will provide you with ideas about how to make your home safer for your family so that you don't have to worry about them.

If you want additional money-saving tips, visit HomeownersNewswire.com or the websites listed in the author's bio at the end of this book.

Have your HVAC system checked regularly. Your HVAC system runs on electricity and, in many cases, also with other substances (like natural gas for your furnace and a refrigerant for your air conditioning unit). These substances are extremely dangerous if they escape the carefully-built confines of your HVAC system. A licensed expert should regularly inspect your HVAC system. At least every 6 months or at a minimum each season change. These appointments are as important as getting a physical for your body.

Clean or replace your HVAC filter regularly and have your ductwork cleaned by a duct cleaning company. Although dust and debris might seem harmless, they can accumulate in your HVAC system (including ductwork) and if not attended to regularly, you potentially increase the risk of a fire if any dust comes into contact with a spark. While this is rare, you don't want to be the rare case when it does happen! Your filters should be changed every 3 months.

Keep your water heater temperature near the recommended setting. Water heater temperatures can be adjusted upward if you want your water to be hotter or downward if you don't want your water to be as hot or safer when children are in the home. While instant hot water is nice, very hot water can potentially burn the skin, especially for children who might want to wash their hands but don't realize that the water is as hot as it is! The recommended heat setting is safe for most homes, especially those with children.

Have a water filtration and purification unit installed. We put a lot of trust into the water utility company to provide us with clean, safe drinking water. But did you know that recent tests by the EPA revealed that millions of Americans are at risk because the water utility companies are simply not able to keep up with water purification requirements? Municipal water filtration costs are rising faster than tax dollars and water bills can charge you; meanwhile, infrastructure is deteriorating. Take matters into your own hands by having a water filtration and purification unit installed in your home. They are far more effective than even those charcoal filter pitchers that people keep in their fridge.

Get an air purification system installed in your home. Nothing is more important than the safety of your family. In a dangerous situation, your first thought is to immediately remove your family. But what if the danger was hidden and low-impact, and its true effect wasn't felt for years? That's what happens with the indoor air quality of your home. Allergens and impurities are inhaled by family members day after day, and since there are no obvious immediate effects, we don't even realize the harm that is taking place. However, years from now your family could face breathing challenges and even increased healthcare costs because of airborne impurities they inhale today. An air purification system can help to proactively keep your family safe from airborne impurities.

Make sure all electrical systems are up to modern safety standards. When you turn on a light switch, you think nothing of it and simply expect the light to turn on. But what you don't realize is that there is a powerful surge of electricity taking place in your walls to power the light. In most cases everything works as it should. However, if you have an older home, a home built with copper wiring, a renovated home, or a home that has been wired by an unlicensed electrical worker then you run the risk of fire or even electrocution every time you turn on a light or plug something into an outlet on the wall.

Put covers over your receptacles. Sometimes light switch or outlet covers go missing. Maybe one cracks and you forget to replace it, or maybe you removed it to paint and aren't sure where it is anymore. Those covers are not just for aesthetics but for safety as well, because they keep little fingers from touching live wires and getting a very dangerous shock!

Get GFCI receptacles. You're probably familiar with the standard double outlet with three holes. They're in nearly every home in America. What you might not know is that more and more homes are turning some or all of those receptacles into GFCI receptacles, which look similar but also have a red and a black button on them. These GFCI receptacles are built to protect your family from electric shock if they happen to be using an electronic item (such as an electric shaver or a hair dryer) and there is a surge or the device falls into water.

Add waterproofing to your home. During winter or a heavy rain, moisture can work its way through nearly-invisible cracks in your foundation. You might not notice it at first but, over time, it gets worse. It not only damages your home, something worse happens: mold develops. Mold is dangerous for your family to breath (in fact, visible mold can even lead to a home being condemned and unlivable!) Protect your family from that risk by getting an expert to provide basement waterproofing to help protect your family from mold.

Want to make your home even safer? We've given you a few ideas here but there are many others. Get in touch with us and we'll send out one of our experts to advise you on some additional ways to make your home safer for your family.

WAYS TO SAVE MONEY IN YOUR HOME

Owning a home can be expensive. It seems like the utility companies are always raising prices for your water, sewer, gas, and electricity.

In this chapter we'll look at some of our top money-saving ideas for your home. These are the same ideas we share with homeowners when we are in their home and they ask us how they can save money on their home.

If you want additional money-saving tips, visit HomeownersNewswire.com or the websites listed in the author's bio at the end of this book.

Close your windows and doors when running your HVAC system. It's simple. If you want your home to be a different temperature than outside, you need to shut the outdoors out and allow your HVAC system to bring the temperature to a comfortable level. If it's really hot outside, draw the curtains or blinds to keep the interior of your house shaded.

Check your weather-stripping. Your house is not air-tight. The windows, doors, and vents that connect the inside to the outside are fitted to the insulation and walls. However, the seal between them is not always perfect, so caulking or rubber weather-stripping is needed to seal them up. This weather-stripping deteriorates every few years so you should check and replace it. If you haven't checked these things in a few years, chances are, it's time to do so.

Don't run your system when you don't need it. Depending on where you live and the time of year, you may not need to run your furnace during the day when no one is home, and you may not need to run your air conditioner at night when everyone is sleeping. Turn off the HVAC system when you don't need it. Or, better yet, install a programmable thermostat so you can adjust the settings automatically. Don't be afraid of this technology like this. It's designed to help us manage our home more efficiently.

Clean your HVAC air filter often and replace it regularly. Your HVAC system pushes warm or cool air through the filter and then through the ducts and into each room of your home. The dirtier your filter is, the harder your HVAC system has to work to push the air through. Cleaning or replacing your filter regularly will keep the airflow moving and will lower your energy bill. (Not to mention, you'll enjoy a healthier lifestyle because your air will be free of dust and debris, and a healthier lifestyle is also less costly in terms of medical bills.) Consider this, you left your home spotless and went on vacation for a week. When you come home, do you find the same spotless house? No! Dust is everywhere. Imagine how dusty/dirty your HVAC ducts are? Imagine if you could see what you're breathing in.

Turn down your water heater when you will be away. Your water heater takes power to run so that it can produce hot water as soon as you need it. However, you may not always need it. If you will be away for a weekend or longer, turn your water heater down so you don't have to pay for the energy required to keep your water hot while you are away, or talk to us about an on-demand tank-less water heater when it comes time for a replacement.

Manage the heat and humidity in your attic. If you've ever had to climb into your attic in the summer, you know it gets VERY hot up there! And in the winter, especially in snowy climates, it gets very humid. This not only makes it harder and costlier to get a comfortable temperature in your home, the heat and humidity can also cause long-term damage (including rot and mold). An attic fan and an attic humidistat can regulate the temperature and humidity to keep your attic at a more moderate temperature. Just because it's out of sight doesn't mean it should be out of mind. You may not notice the difference in your house but you may notice the difference in your heating and cooling bill, plus you'll notice a difference 3-10 years down the road when your attic continues to be comfortable and dry.

Install surge protection. Chances are, you invest money in your valuable electronics. But did you know that an electrical surge can permanently damage those electronics? All electricity coming into your house surges throughout each the day but sometimes those surges can be quite dramatic (especially in a lightning strike or when the power comes back on after it goes out). Unfortunately, not all home insurance covers all power surges. The best solution is to install a whole-home surge protection (NOT those ineffective surge protecting power bars). You'll save money the very first time a surge runs through the neighborhood, destroying everyone else's electronics except yours.

Install a sump pump. Nothing is worse than waking up in the middle of a stormy night and hearing water rushing into your basement from a backed up storm sewer or overloaded weeping tiles. A sump pump removes water before it can enter your home, helping to keep your basement dry. This investment will save you so much money and heartache. This one I lived through personally.

Have your water heater inspected, serviced, and replaced regularly. It's easy to forget about your water heater as long as there is hot water flowing. But older water heaters run less efficiently (and more costly) and are at risk of "bursting". You don't want gallons upon gallons of hot water spilling out all over your basement floor. So have an expert service your water heater regularly. This should be checked yearly.

Install an automated thermostat. One great way to save money is to only raise the temperature in your home when you need it warmer, and lower it when sleeping and when away. The problem is, it's easy to forget to make these adjustments. Fortunately, an automated thermostat—whether one with pre-set adjustments or one of those cutting-edge Wi-Fi-enabled "learning" thermostats that learn your routines and can be controlled by your mobile device and allow you to adjust the temperature conveniently, saving you money.

Want to save money in your home? We've given you a few ideas here, but there are so many others. Get in touch with us and we'll send out one of our experts to advise you on some additional ways to save money!

WAYS TO MAKE YOUR HOME STRESS-FREE

Life can sometimes be stressful enough, even at the best of times. Owning a home can make life even more stressful!

Imagine waking up to a funny sound… Only to discover that your water heater has burst all over your newly-renovated basement.

Imagine arriving home one cold winter evening… Only to discover that your HVAC system isn't working properly and now your home is freezing cold.

Imagine lying awake at night, knowing you have an early and very important day at work tomorrow… Only to hear the drip-drip-drip of a leaky faucet.

If you want additional stress-eliminating ideas, visit HomeownersNewswire.com or the websites listed in the author's bio at the end of this book.

Have an expert check your HVAC system at least twice a year. Your HVAC system is a complex system that can produce both hot and cold air. So, around the time when you switch it over from hot to cold or cold to hot (in the spring and the fall) have a licensed expert check your HVAC system for safety and comfort factors that will help to ensure your system runs at maximum efficiency all season long. The last thing you want is to get home and discover that your furnace wasn't running while you were at work, and now your pipes might be frozen and your house is cold. You don't want to deal with that AND call an HVAC professional. So be proactive about it.

Have an expert check your home's electrical system at least once a year. Your home's electrical system powers everything that makes life comfortable and convenient. However, over time, this system can degrade or become less safe to you. Perhaps your electronic needs change and you find yourself plugging more things in, maybe a receptacle or light switch stops working, or maybe you're worried about electrical fires. An expert can help you solve the little problems (like a receptacle that stops working) and prevent bigger problems (like an electrical fire) from happening.

Have an expert check your home's plumbing system at least once a year. Your plumbing system brings in fresh water from the supply (usually your municipal freshwater system or a well). This water is under pressure, which mean that your plumbing can spring leaks. Not only that but in the winter, your pipes could be at risk for freezing. Avoid leaky pipes (and the costly mess that comes with it) by having a plumber inspect your pipes and faucets every year.

Have an expert check your drain and sewer/septic system at least once a year. Your drain system removes wastewater to the municipal sewer system or to your septic system. Over time, these systems can get clogged up (and septic systems can fill). And, the shifting ground or nearby trees can cause serious problems with your drainpipes. An expert should check this at least once a year to clear your lines, empty your septic tank (if applicable), and diagnose any potential drain pipe problems that need to be addressed.

Install a water filtration system in your home. Your water supply may be compromised and you don't even realize it! If you're worried about what your family is drinking, that will cause a lot of stress because you know they need to stay hydrated but you're worried about the quality of that hydration. Water filtration systems will eliminate the stress and worry so you know you're providing the cleanest, healthiest drinking water for your family.

Install a whole home surge protector. Power surges happen often. Most of them are relatively harmless. However, more powerful surges can take place, especially during a storm or after a power outage. When that happens, your valuable electronics could be permanently damaged (and it may not be covered by your home insurance). A whole home surge protector provides you with the best protection against surges. (Note: those surge protector power strips will not always do the job! A whole home surge protector is built to withstand the electronics-damaging surges).

Install a whole home generator. One of the most stressful things to experience is a power outage. You don't realize how much you rely on power until the power goes out! Then you wonder: will it

45

come back on? How long will it take? Will my food spoil? Will my family still be warm or will my pipes freeze if it doesn't come on in time? End the stress with a whole home generator that is connected right to your home's power system. You'll never worry about outages again… and your home will be the only one on the block that's all lit up even though the rest of your neighbors' houses are dark!

Want to make your home stress-free? We've given you a few ideas here but there are many others. Get in touch with us and we'll send out one of our experts to advise you on some additional ways to help you make your home stress-free.

PART 3.

A QUICK DIVE INTO YOUR HOME'S SYSTEMS AND HOW TO ENSURE THAT YOUR HOME IS AS SAFE AND COMFORTABLE AS POSSIBLE

You're enjoying an evening at home when suddenly you hear a strange noise… you think it might be coming from your basement. Is it the HVAC system? The water heater? The circuit panel?

Knowledge is power. When you read this part of the book, you'll be equipped to understand your home and make the right decisions to keep your home functioning in the best condition, plus you'll get some ideas about how to improve your home, too!

YOUR HOME'S SYSTEMS

This chapter gives you a quick, friendly overview about your home's system so you can understand how everything works together to help your family enjoy a safe and comfortable home.

Most homes in America have an HVAC system, a plumbing system, and an electrical system... but where does it start and how does it work together?

Let's Review:

- **Your HVAC system** provides you with heating, cooling, and air flow (ventilation).
- **Your electrical system** powers your home.
- **Your plumbing system** brings water in to your home.
- **Your drain/sewer/septic system** removes wastewater from your home.

These main systems work together to ensure that your home is as safe and comfortable as possible.

In most cases, these systems start with a source provided by nature or by your local utility company. For example:

- Your HVAC system may be supplied by natural gas or electricity, which is provided by your local utility company. Many homes have a furnace that is run by electricity but uses natural gas to provide the heat, and an air conditioning unit powered by electricity. Some homes have other methods of heating, including electrical or oil.
- Your electrical system may connect to a local electrical supply provided by a utility company.
- Your plumbing system may connect a freshwater supply from a local government-supplied water source or a well, and it may connect your sewer drain to a government-maintained sewer system or a septic system.

There may be some exceptions to the concepts above but those are the most common.

Once you receive the gas, water, and power from the supplying source, they connect to your house and are routed to the appropriate systems by pipes (in the case of gas or water) or wires (in the case of electricity).

- Your HVAC system brings in natural gas and/or electricity to warm and/or cool your home.
- Your electrical system runs wires inside your walls to light switches and outlets (also called receptacles) so that there's power whenever you need it.
- Your plumbing system runs water through pipes inside your walls to the faucets, so you can turn on the tap and get water.
- Your sewer line drains wastewater through the drains to a local sewer line or to a septic tank or septic field.

All of these systems work (mostly) behind the scenes—in your walls and under your cupboards, in wires above the street, or in pipes below the street—to keep your home comfortable. And you barely notice them (unless they stop working for whatever reason).

For the most part, you don't need to know the details of how they work because it can take years of training and qualification to fully understand it all. However, it's helpful to know what's happening behind the scenes in your home so you can take action quickly if you want to make a change or if you encounter a problem with your home.

On the pages that follow, we've shared some of the ways that you can make your home safer and more comfortable:

STRATEGIES FOR YOUR SAFETY AND COMFORT

In the last chapter you read about the main systems in your home that keep your home safe and comfortable for your family: from heating and cooling to electricity, from plumbing to drains, these system work 'round the clock to make sure your home is as safe and comfortable as possible.

When people need an expert to work on these systems they call us. But these aren't the only things in your house that contribute to your family's safety and comfort. In fact, there are many other home safety and comfort strategies (and you may be aware of some of them)... well, we can help you with these as well.

Our team of experts specializes in all the strategies, systems, techniques and services that can ensure your home is safe, comfortable, and beautiful, while also retaining its value AND helping to protect the environment.

On the next several pages are just a few of the most popular services that our team of experts can do. If it has to do with your home, we can probably do it!

Check out the strategies on the next few pages and see if you need any of these right now, or if any of them inspire you to think about getting some work done. Perhaps simply by reading this you think, "Oh! I want that in my home!" or, "Oh! I didn't realize that this needed to be maintained." Then give us a call.

And don't worry—you don't need to know ahead of time if one of these services is right for you. Our experts can help you figure out if one of the services and strategies on the next pages will help to make your family safer and more comfortable.

So turn the page, and think about what you need in your home... AND start dreaming about how you could even make some improvements in your home that weren't thinking about before.

We'd love to help you with any of these...

HVAC INSTALLATION AND REPAIRS

Heating, Ventilation, and Air Conditioning (HVAC) systems should help you achieve an optimal temperature in your home by warming your home when it's cold outside and by cooling your home when it's warm outside. HVAC systems also move air around your home to keep it from becoming stale and to make sure fresh air is delivered to all rooms in your home.

An HVAC expert can repair your existing systems and make sure it is in optimal working condition. An HVAC expert can also install a new system, including high efficiency systems and/or systems that use special filters to clean the air and reduce allergens around your home.

ELECTRICAL REPAIRS AND RENOVATIONS

The wires in your home remain unseen as they deliver power to receptacle and lights. However, over time, they may stop working. Perhaps a circuit gets overloaded, or the house shifts and pulls the wire from an outlet, or maybe during a renovation contractor accidentally cuts through a wire, or perhaps a receptacle burns out from dust or extreme use.

Along with electrical repairs, you may have different electrical needs. Electrical needs of families change over time. Perhaps you need more receptacles now that more family members are charging phones, tablets, and laptops, than you needed years ago.

A licensed electrician can help you by repairing the wiring and receptacles that are no longer working and by rewiring your home in a renovation to ensure that your changing electrical needs are met.

PLUMBING REPAIRS AND RENOVATIONS

There is a lot of water going into your kitchen and bathrooms. From sinks to dishwashers to water dispenser supply lines; from bathtubs to showers to toilets, all of these pipes are under pressure, which can lead to leaking or bursting. An expert can inspect these lines from time to time to make sure they remain intact, and an expert can repair them if they leak or burst.

Or, perhaps you are planning to remodel your kitchen or bathroom. Well, moving any of your fixtures or appliances that need water will mean a plumbing expert should be involved to move the pipes where you need them to go.

DRAIN CLEARING

If your drains aren't clearing, it's a hassle. It could be from a clog in the pipes caused by something that was inadvertently put down the drain, or it could be from a tree root or bend in the pipes that can happen over time.

While there are harsh chemicals that some people try to flush down their drains, it's really much safer to simply call an expert who can take care of it right away. Those harsh chemicals can be extremely dangerous to handle (or even inhale!) and may not always solve the problem.

An expert, though, can safely identify the problem (including the real problem, which may not be solved by harsh chemicals) and can clear your drains and, if necessary, recommend any repairs to keep it from happening again.

WATERPROOFING

Basements are built strong but they can still crack over time, allowing moisture to get in. This can result in mildew, mold, and even flooding! Unfortunately, some insurance companies don't cover all types of basement flooding or mold, depending on the cause.

The best solution is to have an expert assess your basement and recommend a waterproofing solution that gives you the confidence that your basement will remain warm and dry all year 'round.

SURGE PROTECTORS

Power surges through your electrical wires all the time. Usually those surges are minimal and your electronics can handle the surge. But sometimes the surges can become too much for your electronics. This can especially happen during a lightning strike, or right after a power failure when the power comes back on. During a major surge, a lot of electricity surges through the wires and can permanently destroy your electronics. (Your home insurance may or may not cover the damage caused by these surges, and those surge protector strips are inadequate for the most damaging surges.)

Contact an expert and ask about whole home surge protectors. These surge protectors are designed to protect all the electronics in your home and give you the confidence that your home is protected and you won't be inconvenienced in the next surge.

SUMP PUMP

In a heavy rain, the water that collects around your house will drain into your weeping tiles and ideally flow away from your house. However, in a very heavy rainfall, or if your weeping tiles are degraded, or if the municipal sewer system backs up, you can potentially get flooding in your basement.

A sump pump is designed to help protect against this flooding by collecting any backed up water and pumping it far away from your house.

I believe that a sump pump is a recommended device for every home, because you never know when the next rainfall, snowfall, or sewer back-up is going to happen.

An expert can install a sump pump and you'll have the peace of mind that your home is now protected against flooding or water damage.

SOLAR

Electricity is costly and it seems like the costs are always rising! Wouldn't it be nice to minimize your electricity costs by using a free source that is also ecologically friendly?

That's where solar comes in. Solar power is free power from the sun, and it's energy that comes freely every single day of the year! Now, you can harness that power and enjoy the savings you'll get from a lower electricity bill! Plus, you'll love knowing that you are just a little less dependent on non-renewable energy sources.

An expert can advise you on the best solutions for solar power and help you understand where solar energy collectors can go, how to store and use solar power, and how to ensure that your home is not only safe and comfortable but also helping to contribute to an environment that your children's children can enjoy!

GENERATORS

If you've ever been annoyed by a power outage, or hated the inconvenience of not having power, or worried that your food might spoil in the fridge, then a whole home generator is the answer. A whole home generator connects to your home's electrical system and will run as soon as the power goes out, providing you with power even when the rest of your neighborhood is dark.

Your family will be comfortable, your fridge will keep running (so food won't spoil), and your sump pump will have power.

An expert can install a generator to your home's electrical system. If you ever need to sell, just imagine how much more valuable your home will be to prospective buyers when they see that the house will never be without power.

DUCT CLEANING

Running through the floors and walls of your home are ducts that deliver hot or cold air from your furnace and/or air conditioning system to each room of your home.

Over time, dust and airborne debris can build up inside these ducts (yes, even if your HVAC system has a filter). The dust can blow out of your vents around each room, making it difficult to breathe and making your house dusty. Any cigarette smoke or pet dander can be blown around your home through your ducts, too, even if you're careful about where you smoke or where your pets go.

All of these airborne particles can make breathing difficult, and can make your home extra dusty especially for allergy sufferers.

The solution is to have your ducts cleaned regularly—at least once a year—by an expert who has the tools and strategies to do a thorough job. Too many people have their ducts cleaned infrequently but you'll love the difference it makes.

It can also lower your energy bill by reducing the amount of dust that your furnace filter has to collect (which reduces the amount of work that your furnace has to do to warm your house).

HOME SECURITY

We've talked a lot in this book about keeping your home safe for your family, and you already know that dangers lurk everywhere! Not only is water quality and air quality impacting your home's safety but don't forget about dangers from outside too!

You only need to watch the news for a few minutes to know that it's getting crazy out there! It seems like things are getting more and more dangerous every day.

A home security system provides peace of mind to you that your family is protected. From video cameras to keyless entry, from panic buttons to 'round-the-clock monitoring, there are many options and choices to help you ensure your family is safe.

An expert can assess your current situation and advise how best to provide a home security solution that will help your whole family sleep well at night.

HOME INSPECTION

If you're thinking about buying a new home (to live in, as a second home, or as an investment).

Our home inspectors are highly trained experts at investigating the parts of a house that you probably never see! They'll spot hazards, dangers, and opportunities to make your home even safer and more comfortable for your family. They may even help to prevent you from making a bad investment.

Most people think of getting a home inspector during the purchase or sale of a house—and that is the perfect time to have a home inspector look at your house. But you may want to proactively have a home inspector look at your house at other times too, to ensure your house continues to be as safe and comfortable as possible.

Our home inspector experts are highly trained, professional and courteous, and they'll make sure you know exactly what they're looking at AND the specific steps you can take to improve your home.

APPLIANCE REPAIR

Your appliances get a lot of use, and you don't really think about them very much... until they stop working. Your stove, fridge, dishwasher, freezer, or washer and dryer—they're essentials to make sure your family is as comfortable as possible! When they stop working, it's inconvenient, and it can be costly to buy new appliances!

Fortunately, our appliance repair experts are at your service to determine how to get your appliances back into working order as quickly as possible. They'll save you time, money, and inconvenience, and you'll be back to fresh hot food, clean dishes, and clean clothes before you know it!

WATER FILTRATION

Most people don't give a lot of thought to the water that comes out of their taps... but you should. The EPA has found that millions of Americans are at risk of consuming potentially dangerous quantities of various contaminants. Some of the contaminants are in the system and never filtered out, other contaminants are picked up along the miles of pipes to your home.

The water you get from your faucet may taste clean but it could have picked up hazardous chemicals from a factor miles away that the crumbling city water department wasn't able to filter out. It happens more than people realize!

Unfortunately, those charcoal filters in the refillable jugs just don't cut it. They might remove some impurities but won't remove everything that is endangering your family. And bottled water may be sourced from questionable local sources too!

A water filtration and purification system installed by an expert is the best solution to ensuring that your family gets the purest, safest, and best-tasting water possible. There simply is no other way to ensure your family's drinking water is safe.

HOME AUTOMATION

Imagine this: you're headed home from a long day at work. You know the house has been empty all day and it's probably sweltering in there! Or imagine this: Maybe you're headed out of town for the weekend when your spouse asks: did you turn the water heater down?

Good news! Those concerns can be gone for good, making your life so much more convenient and stress-free while also saving you money.

With home automation, you can control your home from your cellphone, including things like your furnace and air conditioner, water heater, stove, and security cameras. Some home automation systems use a high-tech device that learns your family's habits to adjust your home's comfort levels for the way you live.

A home automation expert can help you figure out which tools, devices, and strategies work best for your family.

INDOOR AIR QUALITY

If you ever been worried about what your family is breathing then you'll want to look at some Indoor Air Quality (IAQ) strategies for your home. If not, consider this.

From allergens to toxins, dust to dander, there is a lot of impurities in the air. Not all of it is necessarily dangerous right now but many impurities can lead to headaches, allergies, sleeplessness, sinus congestion, and more. You and your family shouldn't have to live with that discomfort when it can so easily be fixed or avoided all together!

Indoor Air Quality experts can help you find the right combination of IAQ strategies for your home and situation. You'll be amazed at how much better you and your family feel when you're breathing easier!

HANDYMAN SERVICES

Projects around the home are never finished! Maybe you want to finish your basement or add another bathroom; maybe you want to fix a door or repair a wall. There are always little projects to do around the house, and maybe you don't have the time, energy, skill or desire to complete these projects yourself (or maybe you're like a lot of people and you just aren't sure if you have the necessary skills to complete the work to the level you want it to be).

Well, now you can finally cross things off that "Honey Do" list once and for all, without having to lift a hammer yourself. It's nice to know that you can always reach out to us for our handyman services and we'll make sure that a qualified expert can help you with any job—small or large.

Who knows, once you get our handyman started around the house, you might continue finding projects to do!

HOME ENERGY AUDITS

Every time another bill comes in the mail, it seems like they're raising the prices of electricity and natural gas. To make matters worse, homes are not always completely energy-efficient. Small design flaws, degraded insulation, or cracks caused by settling can all make your home less energy efficient.

A home energy auditor will go through your home and look at all the ways that your home could be made more efficient—from how your blower motor runs to how your attic is designed, to the age and quality of your caulking and weather stripping.

A home energy audit can save you a lot of money over the years by finding ways to seal up your home to keep the outdoor climate outside and the warm or cool air inside. As of the writing of this book most utility companies are offering at no cost to qualifying homeowners and we can help facilitate you getting an appointment scheduled.

SEPTIC AND SEWER SYSTEMS

When the water runs down the drain or toilet, where does it go? Typically speaking, in municipal areas it will enter a local sewer system, while in less-populated areas your wastewater enters a septic system. (There are exceptions to this rule).

If you need a septic system built for your home, or if you need to have your home connected to a municipal sewer system, an expert should take care of that for you. This is NOT a process you want to deal with on your own.

A properly installed system will be generally free of problems (although you may need occasional drain clearing) but should be checked periodically to ensure that settling hasn't moved or cracked the pipes.

FIRE, WATER, AND SMOKE RESTORATION

Life doesn't always go as planned. Sometimes the unexpected happens.

If your home sustains fire, water, or smoke damage then you'll want a restoration expert to analyze the situation and create a restoration solution for your home.

Different situations may require different solutions (for example, fire damage could lead to unknown dangers with exposed wood or wires, while water damage that is left untreated could lead to mildew or mold). Often, simply scrubbing the impacted area with soap and water isn't enough.

Fortunately, a restoration expert can help you, (regardless of whether the damage is large or small) get your home back into safe, comfortable, and beautiful condition again.

SIDING

When your home is built, it looks beautiful and perfect. But over time, the weather (and other factors) can take their toll. Siding can get dirty, become cracked or broken, or get pulled away from the structure.

Whether you're fixing some broken siding, adding a home addition that needs siding to match the rest of your home, upgrading your existing siding, or adding siding to reface your entire home, a siding expert can take care of it for you so you don't have to deal with it. A siding expert knows exactly what to do to repair or replace the siding, and can advise you on what siding to use to stand up to the demands of your home and lifestyle.

You'll love how your home looks when the siding expert is done! It will look like you've bought an entirely new house!

ROOFING

The roof on your home takes the worst that Mother Nature can dish out. Scorching sun, freezing snow and ice, pounding rain, shearing wind. After a few years of this abuse, your shingles wills start to show wear and tear. Their protective qualities will diminish over time. Some will loosen. Others might tear and come off completely. Soon, you could have rain or snow coming into house through your roof.

A roofing expert can keep your home dry, damage-free and stress-free by making sure your roof is in the best state of repair and fully operational.

They won't just look at the shingles, either. They may be able to help you with the roof boards, heat or humidity problems in your attic, and the waterproofing and flashing around chimneys and pipes.

You'll probably need to change up your shingles every 15-20 years, but you may want a roofing expert to look at your roof more frequently than that to ensure it's in "peak" condition.

AWNINGS

Without any cover, the sun can shine through your windows. Even through curtains or blinds, your house can get extremely hot, and the sun can even fade the furniture, pictures, and paint on the wall. On the hottest days, who wants to sit outside on the back deck in the blistering sun?

Awnings are the answer. Awnings can be placed over windows, doors, and decks. This creates beautiful shade that protects whatever is underneath, keeping your home cool and the colors vibrant (no more faded furniture!), and allows you to enjoy a cool, shaded deck for dinner with the family.

An awnings expert can talk to you about what your needs are and can recommend some of the best solutions to provide shade wherever you need it.

PAINTING

Much of your home is probably painted. You might have wood or wood trim on the outside that are painted, and you probably have many rooms in your house that are painted.

Paint doesn't last. Pain fades with the sun; paint chips and flakes with wear; paint colors go in and out of style; paint can lose its protective qualities (such as any waterproofing/sealing that might occur on a deck or porch). Sometimes you just need a fresh coat of paint for no reason, other than to just look clean and fresh od change the look of a room!

Don't spend your own precious time painting. It's time consuming, messy, smelly, stressful. Instead, talk to a painting expert who can bring in one or more team members and complete a painting job in a fraction of the time, and clean up too. All you're left with is a beautiful, fresh coat of paint!

FLOORING

Your floors take a lot of abuse each and every day. From the moment you move into your home and the movers haul heavy furniture and appliances over it… or every single day when you walk across it, spill things on it, the kids play on it, the pets run on it. Floors stand up to a lot of daily activity. Over time, those floors can show that wear and tear and need to be upgraded.

Maybe you are renovating your home and adding value to it. Maybe your children have grown up and moved out so it's time to reward yourself with floors that are less about durability for children and more about a chic look that matches your new décor.

A flooring expert can advise you on the best flooring for your needs, and even make suggestions about how to improve the look, comfort, and value of your home with the choice of certain flooring types in various rooms. You'll be amazed at how different and fresh your home looks once you have a new floor installed!

INSULATION

Does your home get cold very quickly in the winter, after the furnace shuts off? Does it get hot very quickly in the summer, after the air conditioner shuts off? Perhaps you need to add or upgrade your insulation.

Insulation can be added in floors, walls, ceilings, and attics to help moderate the temperature (while also protecting your home from temperature extremes outside, which could lead to problems like frozen pipes), and can also provide sound insulation to keep your home a quiet sanctuary for you.

Even if your home was built with insulation, it's possible that the insulation has settled or degraded over the years, providing less insulating quality now versus when it was first installed.

An insulation expert can advise you various insulation options that will protect your home and keep your family comfortable.

GARAGE DOORS

Does your home have a garage? Then you may be thinking about changing the door. Those standard one-piece metal doors are very common but can become dented or chipped from heavy use and abuse from the elements. Maybe you are thinking about upgrading your garage door, perhaps to multi-panel garage door or even a beautiful carriage-style door.

If you want to replace or upgrade your existing garage door, an expert can help you find the right one, help you choose the right locks, and also install remote garage door openers for added convenience.

You'll love pulling into your driveway at the end of the day and pressing the button to see your beautiful garage door open to pull your car in.

HOME THEATERS

One of the biggest trends in homes right now is the home theatre. No longer are families content to have one small black and white TV in the living room, like your parents or grandparents! Today, families are setting aside an entire room that is purpose-built for high-tech, home theater entertainment. From sound-proof walls to comfy reclining chairs... from widescreen TVs (or even projectors) to crystal-clear surround sound... your home may not feel complete until you have a beautiful high-tech theater experience built right into your home.

If you're thinking about adding a home theater to your home, an expert will help you figure out how to best achieve the experience you want, and can work with you on your budget to ensure that you get the best experience for your family.

POWER WASHING

You might not notice it but a layer of dust and grime can built up on the outside walls of your home. Because it happens over time, combined with rain and snow, a thick and stubborn layer can build up that won't come off just with a garden hose.

Power washing your home, your deck, and even your driveway will instantly give your home a beautiful, fresh appearance just like when you first moved in to your home. Your house will shine in your neighborhood!

Although some people choose to rent their own equipment, that can be a hassle and a mess. Spend your time doing more important things and let a power washing expert take care of it for you, by cleaning your home's exterior with their high-tech equipment.

You'll be amazed at the difference and, like a lot of our clients, you may want your home power washed each and every year.

GUTTERS AND LEADERS

You may not realize it but your roof covers a wide area of your property. When it rains, or when the snow melts, that's a lot of water that has to go somewhere.

Gutters and leaders work together to move all that water from your roof in a controlled fashion down and away from your home. With gutters in place, water cascades off the roof, down the leaders, and drains a safe distance from the structure. However, without a gutter in place, water would just run off your roof, collect at your foundation, and potentially flood your basement.

If you don't have gutters or leaders, or if yours have been damaged, you should get them fixed as soon as possible. Gutters and leaders should be checked and cleaned regularly, and they may need to be patched, repaired, or replaced if they develop holes or pull away from your home. An expert should look at your gutters and advise you on the best steps to take.

HOME CONSTRUCTION

Are you thinking about doing a major renovation on your existing home… or even having a new home built? Maybe an addition? This is a big undertaking that you should never do yourself. Leave it to the professionals who know the correct steps to take, the permits required, and the best strategies to use in the climate conditions of the area you live.

You do not need to know ahead of time what your full plan is; simply let our home construction expert know what you'd like to do and the expert will walk you through suggestions, steps and timeline, and help put together a plan and budget that fits your needs.

KITCHEN AND BATH REMODELING

Over time, your lifestyle changes: the kids grow up; home design trends and tastes change; maybe you simply want to update and upgrade the rooms you use most often; maybe you're thinking of selling and want a home that looks clean and modern.

Perhaps, like a lot of our clients, you've put up with your kitchen and bath in a certain way for a long time but now your tastes and budget and lifestyle have changed and you're ready to enjoy an upgrade to the beautiful, functional, and stylish kitchen and bath of your dreams!

For any reason (or for no reason at all) you may want to remodel your kitchen and bathroom. There are remodeling strategies for every budget and every lifestyle, from extremely simple plans that can be done in a day or two, all the way up to major remodeling that will create a dramatic difference even in the layout of the room.

A kitchen and bath remodeling expert can explain your options and work with you to find the very best remodeling plan for you.

WINDOW AND DOOR REPLACEMENT

The windows and doors of your home serve important purposes. Not only do the doors let you in and out, they also protect you when locked, plus, a well-chosen door adds a beautiful design touch. Not only do the windows let the sunlight in and allow you to see outside, they also protect you from the outside elements (and as security devices from intruders), plus, well-chosen windows add a beautiful design touch.

Choosing the right windows and doors is not something you can do by spending a few minutes at a home renovation store. There are so many considerations, from the climate where you live to the level of security you want... even to how much sunlight you want coming through the windows.

If it's time to replace your windows and doors, a window and door replacement expert will help you understand your options and will show you the best solutions for your lifestyle and situation.

FENCING

As the saying goes, "good fences make good neighbors." Fences provide you with security and privacy, keeping your family safe and secure, and turning your yard into a beautiful, private retreat.

From metal to plastic to wood, there are many fencing options for every lifestyle and budget. However, there might be other considerations too, such as municipal bylaws, where your property line is, or how you plan to use your yard.

A fencing expert is the best person to speak with about how to add, repair, replace, or upgrade a fence around your front- or backyard. You'll love the impact a fence can have on the look of your home from the street, and on how private it makes your yard feel from inside the fence.

MASONRY

You may not realize it but masonry services can do a lot in and around your home. In fact, once you realize what a masonry expert can do, you'll probably start making a long list!

A masonry expert can improve the strength and structure of your home with brick repairs and replacement, and (in some cases) foundation repair. In your yard, a mason can build retaining walls or install, repair, or replace concrete steps. A masonry expert can create a strong, beautiful, long-lasting driveway and walkway. A masonry expert can create indoor or outdoor fireplaces and patios too! Wherever brick or concrete can be used, a masonry expert can provide a strong, permanent, beautiful solution.

LANDSCAPING

You think about the safety, comfort, and beauty of your home, but remember that the same concepts extend to the land around your structure too.

Landscaping provides functional solutions like grading (to control flooding), as well as aesthetic solutions like gardens, tree-planting, and more.

Landscapers can provide one-time or year-round service to create a beautiful home and yard, and to keep it looking pristine in every season. Do you know which flowers and trees will grow best in the area you live? Do you know which flowers and trees grow best in the sunlight and shaded areas around your home? Do you know how to plant so that you have different flowers in spring, summer and fall? A landscaping expert does and can help!

Using various techniques, a landscaper can create a show stopping front yard that will have your neighbors slowing down to take a longer look, as well as a beautiful, relaxing, and private retreat in your backyard where you'll want to spend more time with your family.

TREE SERVICE

Trees are beautiful and can add tremendous value to your home. Sometimes that value is financial, if you are in an area where trees are a valuable commodity to have on your property. Trees can bring shade and beauty, or squeals of laughter as children climb and play around those trees—they're an asset.

Sure, you have to keep an eye on them, and maybe clean out your gutters a little more often, and rake in the fall, but a tree is wonderful asset to have.

However, trees are living things and like all living things, they need to be cared for. Often, trees can function on their own without a lot of care but if you really want your trees to become even more beautiful and valuable to your home, a tree service is the way to go.

A tree service expert can provide you with strategies and resources to create a stronger and more beautiful tree. They can recommend a fertilizer blend if the tree doesn't have the right color, or they can prune a tree if necessary, or even safely remove a tree if it needs to be removed.

PEST CONTROL

You're enjoying a peaceful evening with your family when suddenly you hear something… a scratching in the walls? Or maybe something running across the floor. Pests! Pests can include insects or rodents—anything unwanted.

Pests are attracted into your home for a variety of reasons, whether it's because of the warmth in the fall and winter, or because of food crumbs on the ground that were missed when sweeping.

A pest control expert can identify what pests are the problem, assess the extent of the problem, and give you some strategies to have them removed. You do not want to live with pests in your house so if you have any, talk to a pest control expert right away.

LOCKSMITHING

When we lock ourselves out of the house, we call a locksmith. that's what many people think of when they think of a locksmith. But a locksmith does so much more than that! A locksmith can not only help you when you lock yourself out of your home or car but can also help you figure out your security needs for your home and lifestyle.

For example, perhaps you want something more than a standard doorknob lock for your front and back door—a locksmith can advise you on you other types of locking mechanisms and home security strategies to give you the peace of mind that your family will be safe.

Our expert locksmiths will help you figure out the best plan for you, and may even be able to help you with other locks in your home that you didn't consider—from a gun safe to a small vault for your valuables.

JUNK REMOVAL

Over time it's easy to accumulate junk that you don't need. But after a thorough spring cleaning or after a renovation, you may have some junk around your home that you need carted away. Old appliances, building materials, an old chair, maybe stuff that the kids didn't take with them when they went to college.

And maybe it's too much to drag to the curb. So, what do you do with it? Getting rid of it yourself requires a truck, and an afternoon, and then you have to figure out if you can take it all to the dump or if some of it has to go somewhere else, like to a recycling center.

But our junk removal expert is a fast and simple phone call away and can take care of all it for you. You won't get dirty or strain your back loading it into the truck, and you don't have to worry about whether there's a dump fee or if it will all fit. You'll have so much room in your house and garage when you're done!

MAID SERVICES

How much time do you spend cleaning each week? Chances are, you and your family spend a lot of time each week cleaning, but it's often time you would much rather spend doing something else—like going to the park, walking the dog, hanging out in the backyard, or visiting friends and family.

More and more of our clients are looking for maid services to clean for them. When you consider how valuable your time is, and how precious it is to spend with family, then having someone else come in and take care of the cleaning is a valuable benefit that gives you more time with your family. Moreover, you'll maintain the safety, comfort, and value of your home by keeping up with some cleaning that you might normally be too busy to take care of.

Whether you want help each week or just once in a while, when you need someone to do some light cleaning or a thorough top-to-bottom cleaning of your home, you'll love how convenient it is to have our expert maid services take care of it for you.

DECKS AND PATIOS

Imagine this: the sun is shining, it's a beautiful day outside, and even though it's hot, there is some welcome shade on your gorgeous deck or patio. You and your family sit in the shade and enjoy the weather, perhaps watch the kids or grandkids or pets play in the backyard as you sip a cool beverage and listen to the birds.

A deck or patio is an invaluable asset to have in your home. It's a quiet, relaxing place to enjoy your family and visitors, perhaps barbecue or read a book.

Our deck and patio expert can look at your front or back yard and advise you on your best choices for a deck or patio. Many of our clients are getting a small deck in the front and a larger deck and perhaps a patio in the back—it just depends on your lifestyle.

If you have a deck already, our expert can show you how to maintain and improve it or how to convert it to be almost maintenance free, to keep it comfortable for you all year long.

LAWN IRRIGATION

You know your lawn needs to be watered, but do you know how much or how often? What about during each season? It may also depend on the type of grass you have and the exact make-up of your soil and whether some of your lawn is in shade or direct sun.

Every lawn is different. But for most people, watering their lawn is something they do as an afterthought... on a weekend... if they remember.

A lawn irrigation expert knows exactly what your lawn needs: from the amount of water to the frequency, based on a number of factors. A lawn irrigation expert can install an irrigation system without tearing up your entire lawn in your yard to ensure that your yard gets all the water it needs, when it needs it.

Just think: you never have to water your lawn again, and you never have to be embarrassed about having the driest, brownest lawn in the neighborhood. A lawn irrigation expert will help you find the right solution to have the greenest lawn on your street.

CARPET CLEANING

Carpets can be a beautiful, functional way to have a comfortable room. Instead of a hard, cold floor, you walk across a comfortable inviting carpet.

However, carpets are also basically giant filters that suck in all the dirt, dust, debris, dander, hair, germs, and other particles that land on the floor. Although beautiful, over time your carpet can pick up a lot of unpleasant things and can start to look and smell unpleasant.

If you have a carpet cleaning expert to clean your carpets, you'll be amazed at the difference. They'll draw out all the dirt and grime and return your carpets to near new condition. You'll feel like you're walking again on brand new carpets. Not only will your carpets be clean and look amazing, you won't be stirring up that debris by walking on the carpets, and you'll prolong the life of your carpets too! It just makes so much sense to hire a carpet cleaning expert.

DRIVEWAY REPAIR AND SEALING

Your driveway is a large flat surface, usually made of concrete or asphalt. It looks beautiful when it's first installed but over time it can start to deteriorate. Between the weight of your car, plus the movement of the ground due to extreme temperatures, your driveway can form cracks and dips, and can even degrade to the point where large chunks come out. When this happens, grass starts to grow in your driveway and the cracks collect rainwater or snow, which leads to further degradation.

To avoid this, you should have a driveway repair and sealing expert regularly inspect your driveway and recommend a treatment to take care of your driveway. They may want to seal it now, as a proactive measure against further cracks, or they may do a large repair first and then seal it if your driveway needs it.

You'll be amazed at how great your driveway looks when it's been repaired and sealed; it can really make the exterior of your house pop!

CHIMNEY CLEANING AND REPAIR

Chances are, you don't think very much about your chimney. However, you'll probably want to think about it for the safety and comfort of your family.

Your chimney—from a woodstove, fireplace, or even your furnace—is meant to draw smoke or carbon monoxide out of, and away from, your home. Over time, though, your chimney collects debris on the inside making it more difficult for the chimney to operate.

A chimney that is ignored for too long can even become blocked up completely, and this can force the smoke or carbon monoxide into your home, endangering your family. Do not ignore your chimney!

Our chimney experts can inspect your chimney and will advise you on the best strategy to clean and repair it to keep it in safe working order.

SEASONAL CHECKLISTS TO MAKE YOUR HOME SAFER AND MORE COMFORTABLE

Spring, Summer, Fall, and Winter. The seasons happen like clockwork. We look forward to various things in each season, like events, holidays, vacations, the start of the school year, etc.

The seasons may bring new opportunities, adventures and changes for your family but they also bring changes to your house. If you want to ensure that your home is as safe and comfortable as it can be all year 'round, then there are a few simple tasks you should do around your house each season. These tasks are easy and fun, and many can be completed in an evening or on a weekend, especially if the whole family pitches in. Completing these tasks every season will make sure that your home is safe, comfortable, and well-maintained all year 'round.

SPRING
In spring, focus on freshening up your home and protecting your property against the season's strong winds and rains.

Outdoor tasks
☐ Clean gutters and downspouts. Learn how to maintain your gutters.
☐ Inspect roof and chimney for cracks and damage.
☐ Touch up peeling or damaged paint.
☐ Wash all windows, inside and out.
☐ Install screens on windows and doors.
☐ Clean outdoor furniture and air out cushions.
☐ Service your lawn mower.
☐ Fertilize your lawn.

Indoor tasks
☐ Test smoke and carbon monoxide detectors when you set clocks forward.
☐ Change the air filter for your furnace.

☐ If your basement has a sump pump, test it by dumping a large bucket of water into the basin of the sump pump. This should activate the sump pump. If it does not switch on, or if it's not pumping water, it may need to be serviced by a professional. Also, check for and remove any debris in the pump hole and make sure there are no leaks.

☐ Wash and change seasonal bedding.

☐ Dust blinds and vacuum curtains throughout your house.

☐ Clean kitchen and bathroom cabinets and throw away outdated food, medicine, and cosmetics.

☐ Inspect attic fan to make sure there are no animal nests, then test.

☐ Have air conditioner outside unit professionally inspected.

☐ Test whole home generator for proper function.

☐ Test panel circuit breakers.

☐ Test all home GFCI receptacles.

☐ Change water filters.

SUMMER

In summer, complete the following projects to keep your yard lush and your home cool.

Outdoor tasks

☐ Walk around your home's exterior and slide open crawl space vents at the foundation.

☐ Prune trees and shrubs.

☐ Remove lint from dryer exhaust vent with a long, flexible brush.

☐ Uncover central air conditioner or install window air conditioners.

Indoor tasks

☐ Change or clean heating, ventilation, and air conditioning filters. (Consult manufacturer instructions to determine whether you need to change filters more frequently.)

☐ Clean kitchen appliances inside and out, including refrigerator coils.

☐ Maintain clean drains by adding a half-cup of baking soda, followed by a half-cup of white vinegar. After 10 minutes, flush with boiling water.

☐ Drain or flush water heater.

☐ Test all GFCI receptacles.

☐ Change any water filters for water quality.

FALL

In fall, prepare your home and yard for cooler temperatures, falling leaves, and more hours spent indoors.

Outdoor tasks

☐ Clean gutters and downspouts. Make sure all drainage areas are unblocked by leaves and debris. (Consider installing gutter guards to make the job a lot easier.)

☐ Inspect your roof, or hire a licensed professional to examine your roof for wear and tear. If the shingles are curling, buckling, or cracking, replace them. If you have a lot of damage, it's time to replace the entire roof. Also, check the flashing around skylights, pipes, and chimneys. If you have any leaks or gaps, heavy snow and ice will find its way in.

☐ Run your generator through a test cycle. Tune up if needed.

☐ Check basement and crawl spaces for any cracks or signs of moisture that need to be sealed.

☐ Close or install storm windows.

☐ Remove hoses from spigots. Drain them, coil them up, and store them flat, preferably indoors.

☐ Store outdoor furniture and cushions.

☐ Test all outside floodlights and motion sensors.

☐ Use a screwdriver to probe the wood trim around windows, doors, railings, and decks. Use caulk to fill the holes or completely replace the wood.

☐ To prevent exterior water pipes from bursting when the weather gets below freezing, turn off the valves to the exterior hose bibs. Run the water until the pipes are empty. Make sure all the water is drained from the pipes. (If not, the water can freeze up and damage the pipes.)

- ☐ You may also choose to paint the exterior of your home because lower humidity and cooler (but not yet cold) temperatures make fall a good time to paint.

Indoor tasks

- ☐ Check grout and silicone in bathtubs and showers, and seal if needed.
- ☐ Have furnace professionally inspected.
- ☐ Test sump pump for property operation. (Check the battery back-up too!)
- ☐ Change the air filter for your furnace.
- ☐ Inspect ducts and decide if duct cleaning is needed (recommendation: do this before major allergies hit!)
- ☐ Check indicator lights on all home surge protectors.
- ☐ Test all home GFCI receptacles.
- ☐ Change water filters for water quality.
- ☐ Test smoke alarms and carbon monoxide detectors.
- ☐ Vacuum the lint from the clothes dryer.
- ☐ Vacuum condenser coils to increase energy efficiency.

WINTER

In winter, enjoy energy-efficient warmth and the fruits of your home-maintenance labors. Use this time of the year to thoroughly clean and care for your home's interior while taking a few precautionary measures on the outside.

Outdoor tasks

- ☐ Walk around your home's exterior and check the crawl space vents located at the foundation. Close any that are open.
- ☐ Protect your central air conditioning unit with a cover.
- ☐ Remove and store window air conditioners.
- ☐ Clean and store garden tools.
- ☐ Move snow shovels and snow blowers to a convenient spot. Stock your ice melting compound to melt ice on walkways.

Indoor tasks

- ☐ Change or clean furnace filters.

- ☐ Clean kitchen appliances inside and out, including refrigerator coils.
- ☐ Maintain clean drains by adding BioClean product.
- ☐ Check around your foundation for moisture and cracks that are expanding inside and outside.
- ☐ Inspect your roof for loose tiles or shingles and for signs of leaks around vents, skylights, and chimneys.
- ☐ Touch up any interior or exterior paint that is cracking or peeling.
- ☐ Clean out gutters and downspouts to remove leaves and other blockages.
- ☐ Cleanout the chimney to remove buildup of flammable substances. Have a professional look at your chimney every year to prevent a fire hazard during the winter months.
- ☐ Drain the water heater until it is clear of sediment and then refill with clean water.
- ☐ Clean grill and fan blades on exhaust fans.
- ☐ Flush your garbage disposal with hot water and baking soda.
- ☐ Lubricate the hinges and moving parts on all doors and windows, including your garage door.
- ☐ Shampoo carpets and wax floors.

PART 4.

COMMON PROBLEMS AND WHAT TO DO ABOUT THEM

When your furnace stops working, you know it's time to call in an expert who can repair or replace it. But there are many times when you have issues around your house that you may not even realize can be fixed by an expert! You just learn to live with the inconvenience, cost or risk… and perhaps you just don't know that an expert can take care of it for you quickly.

In this part of the book we'll look at a number of common problems and situations around your house and you'll discover that an expert may be able to help you with more than you realize!

At the very end of this part of the book I've provided a convenient checklist that you can use to go through your home to identify areas that need work.

COMMON PROBLEMS AND CONCERNS AROUND YOUR HOME

When your furnace stops working, you know it's time to call in an expert who can repair or replace it. There are often little things that need work but you just learn to live with them.

- Maybe an power receptacle stops working.
- Maybe there are hot and cold spots in the house.
- Maybe your laundry room is just too dark.
- Maybe you never realized the danger of a power surge and the damage it could do to your electronics.

Those are just a few examples of the things that we live with every day. We just learn to work around the power receptacle that stops working, or we just learn to squint when we're doing laundry.

But it doesn't have to be that way. Your home is your castle and it should be the place where life is simple and convenient, not where you have to work around problems.

So, go through this part of the book and see if any of these situations are happening in your home.

Also, I always advise that all members of the household go through this at the same time—perhaps after dinner one evening. It won't take long. But the reason I suggest this is: you may not notice the same things that your spouse or kids notice.

For example, one of my customers went to his work every day while his wife stayed home to look after their two young children. He thought his home's temperature was fine but his wife pointed out that the children's playroom was never quite as warm as the rest of the house. He didn't realize because he often played with his children outside in the evening rather than in their playroom. The wife knew; the husband didn't!

Or another client where the parents thought the house was problem-free but the teenagers said, "oh, the bathroom sink has been clogged for months."

So, sit down with your family and briefly go through this part of the book to see if any of these situations are happening in your home right now.

COMMON PROBLEMS ABOUT YOUR HOME'S TEMPERATURE

In this chapter we'll look at common problems that you may face about your home's temperature, explore some of the possible causes and what you can do about them. In some cases, we'll give you ideas and tips to help you know what to do; in other cases you may need to contact a licensed expert to help you.

Due to variations in homes from one area to the next, we have provided the most general recommendations here. If you are ever unsure what the problem is or what to do about it, always have a licensed expert take a look at the situation for you. (Even just calling our office and talking to an expert over the phone may help you narrow down the problem.)

No matter what, always be safe. Your safety and your family's safety are the most important thing so don't try anything that is dangerous or if you are not sure what the outcome might be.

HVAC systems are built safe and to high standards with many safeguards in place, and they are very safe when installed by a licensed professional. However, if you are ever worried about the safety of your family, then leave the house immediately with your children and pets and contact a licensed HVAC expert to help you.

Here are some common problems that homeowners experience around their home with regard to the temperature of the home.

My house is too cold!
- Consider whether this is normal or if it's a new situation. (For example, is your house always cold? It might mean that you need a new or bigger furnace. If it's a new situation, there could be a temporary problem with your furnace.)
- Check that all doors and windows are closed tightly.
- Check the weather-stripping around doors and windows.
- Check to make sure your furnace is running. (Is it plugged in? Is the breaker on your circuit panel in the "on" position?)

- Check the furnace filter to see if it is clean.
- Check to make sure there is nothing blocking the vents.
- Contact a licensed HVAC expert to help you.

My furnace is making an unusual noise.

- If possible, try to narrow down the source of the noise: is it coming from the furnace itself? Is it coming from the ductwork elsewhere in the house?
- If possible, try to narrow down when the noise occurs: does the sound happen consistently? Does it happen only when the furnace is about to turn on to heat the house or about to turn off once your house has reached the right temperature?
- Think about what the noise is: A metallic rattling? A hissing? A buzzing?
- Contact a licensed HVAC expert to help you.

I smell dust or smoke whenever my furnace comes on.

- Check your furnace air filter and clean or replace it if it is dirty.
- If it's clean and you still smell dust or smoke, there may be dust in your ducts that should be cleaned out.
- Contact a licensed HVAC expert to help you.

My house is too hot!

- Consider whether this is normal or if it's a new situation. (For example, is your house always hot? It might mean that you need a new or bigger air conditioner. If it's a new situation, there could be a temporary problem with your air conditioner.)
- Check your air conditioning system to see if it is plugged in and running. If it's plugged in but not running, check the circuit panel and reset the breaker.
- Check the filter to see if it is dirty and needs to be cleaned or replaced.
- Check the ducts and vents to ensure there are no blockages
- Contact a licensed HVAC expert to help you.

COMMON PROBLEMS ABOUT YOUR HOME'S ELECRICAL SYSTEM

In this chapter we'll look at common problems that you may face about your home's electricity, explore some of the possible causes and what you can do about them. In some cases, we'll give you ideas and tips to help you know what to do; in other cases you may need to contact a licensed expert to help you.

My receptacles or fan/lights aren't working!
- Check the light or the electronic device you have plugged into the receptacle. Make sure the light bulb hasn't blown or there isn't something defective with the device itself. (For example, try the bulb in another light in a different room, or try plugging your electronic device into a receptacle in a different room.
- Check to see if a circuit needs to be reset, and reset if necessary.
- If neither of these things work, contact an licensed expert.

COMMON PROBLEMS ABOUT YOUR HOME'S PLUMBING SYSTEM

In this chapter we'll look at common problems that you may face about your home's plumbing, explore some of the possible causes and what you can do about them. In some cases, we'll give you ideas and tips to help you know what to do; in other cases you may need to contact a licensed expert to help you.

My faucets are leaking.
- Make sure the taps are fully turned off.
- If your faucet continues to leak, contact a licensed expert.

There's water dripping from a pipe.
- Place a bucket under the drip.
- See if you can locate the source (it may not always be directly under the drip, since a leak may occur at a higher part of the pipe but the water will drip off the lowest part of the pipe).
- Turn off the nearest valve, if there is one, or turn off your home's main water intake valve.

My hot water is not very hot.
- Determine whether another hot water source has recently drained your hot water tank (for example, if you take a shower shortly after doing a large load of laundry).
- Determine whether your water needs have changed recently (such as, if your family of 4 usually has an adequate hot water supply but when you have guests, not everyone gets a hot shower.
- Check to see if your hot water tank's temperature setting is still at the recommended position.

- Check to see if your hot water tank is operating (i.e. if it's a gas powered tank, is the pilot light on?) Restart the system if possible.
- Think about when you last flushed your hot water tank.
- If the setting is where it's always been, and if the tank seems to be operating normally then contact an expert to help you.

COMMON PROBLEMS ABOUT YOUR HOME'S DRAIN/SEWER/SEPTIC SYSTEM

In this chapter we'll look at common problems that you may face about your home's drain/sewer/septic system, explore some of the possible causes and what you can do about them. In some cases, we'll give you ideas and tips to help you know what to do; in other cases you may need to contact a licensed expert to help you.

My toilet isn't draining.
- Plunge your toilet then dump a bucket of water into the toilet (be careful to avoid spillage!)
- If that doesn't work, contact an expert to help you.

My sink or bathtub drain isn't draining.
- Check to make sure there is nothing blocking the drain, including the plug itself, debris, hair, a toy, etc.
- If possible, pour baking soda then vinegar down the drain. (You should only do this if the sink or tub is not too full. If you can get to the drain easily then you should try this.)
- If those don't work, contact an expert to help you.

CHECKLIST OF COMMON PROBLEMS
AROUND YOUR HOME

Homes need a regular check-up, just like we do, to ensure proper efficiency. Use this checklist to help you identify your home systems that could be made safer and more comfortable for your family.

☐ Are you concerned about utility bills going up while your furnace, boiler, water heater, air conditioner age?

☐ Does your family suffer from allergies or other breathing troubles?

☐ Are you frustrated by temperature differences (e.g., some areas of your home are hot while other areas are cold)?

☐ Have the ducts in your home been cleaned recently to remove dust and allergens?

☐ Can you control your thermostat when you're away; or do you get worried about unnecessary heating bills or frozen pipes?

☐ Has your heating and/or cooling equipment become annoyingly loud and noisy during start-up or shutdown?

☐ Do you get frustrated because the house is NEVER the right temperature during the winter or summer?

☐ Does your attic get very hot and humid during the summer months; or worse, have you detected mold in your attic?

☐ Are you concerned about switches or plugs that are warm to the touch, and stressed that it could cause issues; are there any plugs that feel loose when plugging or unplugging something?

☐ Are you aggravated by a breaker that keeps tripping?

☐ Have you ever had to endure the expense and hassle of replacing appliances or electronics due to a power surge, or your home being hit by lightning?

☐ Are there areas in the home where you have to run extension cords and could use another outlet so it does not cause a safety risk?

☐ Has there been any annoyingly slow-draining sinks, tubs, or toilets? (Note: even if they're working right now, have they occurred within the last five years?)

☐ Does your home suffer from hard water causing a white build up on your plumbing; and are you worried about the impact on your family's health?

☐ Are you concerned about what your children are drinking when they fill a glass from the tap or brush their teeth?

☐ Do you have that agonizing problem of running out of hot water for showers and baths earlier than you would like?

☐ Are you worried that your basement will be ruined from a sump pump failure due to a power outage?

☐ Are you concerned about your family's health or long term issue because of your basement's damp walls, or mold and musty odors?

☐ Do you experience flickering lights, unexpected dimming or repeatedly burned out bulbs?

If you've checked off any of these, contact Addario's Services Company today to solve this problem for you right away.

PART 5.

HOW TO FIND A TRUSTED EXPERT TO HELP YOU SAVE MONEY, SAVE TIME, ELIMINATE STRESS, AND MAKE YOUR HOME SAFER AND MORE COMFORTABLE FOR YOUR FAMILY

You've determined that your home needs to be serviced by a professional… but who should you hire? At first glance, there seem to be so many home service companies out there. Maybe you're not sure what the difference is, or maybe you're not sure if you should hire a home service company or just get your cousin to fix it because he's handy around the house? In Part 5 of the book you will learn how to make better decisions for your home and find out who is best able to help you make your home safer and more comfortable for your family.

HOW TO MAKE WISE DECISIONS FOR YOUR HOME

Life is busy. You go to work, you go to the grocery store, you take the kids to soccer practice… you barely have time to catch your breath!

For that reason, some aspects of life get put on the backburner. Maybe you don't pursue those hobbies as much as you used to. Maybe you don't get to spend as much time outside as you'd like. Maybe you don't get to visit friends as often as before you had kids or grandkids.

Sometimes, your house takes a backburner too. You're busy making decisions and paying bills and putting dinner on the table and making sure that the dog is fed that you don't always get five minutes to yourself to think about your home.

If that's the case for you, you're not alone. That's very common. The good thing is: your home's systems tend to run themselves for the most part. You don't have to think about them. Instead, you can get on with your life.

But sometimes you do need to think about your home. Maybe your HVAC system doesn't produce as much heat as it used to, or maybe the drain is blocked.

Now what?

Until this point you didn't have to think about your home but all of a sudden it's become a priority. You need your house to be safe and comfortable for your family and when it's not, it's suddenly a priority.

For a lot of people, this can feel overwhelming and even challenging. After all, before this happened you were probably maxed out and busy with other aspects of life, and suddenly this problem in your home takes all of your attention.

It can be overwhelming! You were busy beforehand but then when something happened in your home this just became a priority. The other stuff didn't go away but now you have to squeeze in this more important problem and find a wise solution quickly!

You'll love this (and people tell us that it's the chapter they turn to most often in this book): When you have situation in your home, you can turn to this chapter as a simple way to help you make the best decisions for your home and family. Included in this chapter is a simple step-by-step way to think about the problem and to reach a solution quickly, without a lot of stress.

Think of this as a simple checklist that you run through whenever you encounter a challenge with your home. Simply go through each step in the list below and answer the question, and then go on to the next step. By the time you're done, you'll have a game-plan that is ideally suited to get the problem solved and get your life back on track!

First, identify the situation. For example, maybe the house isn't as warm or cool as it needs to be. Maybe the faucet is dripping. Maybe it's not a critical problem (like a broken HVAC system) but rather you just need to upgrade your bathroom.

Second, identify the source of the problem (if possible). This isn't always possible but if you can, try to trace the source of the problem. Your leaky faucet is probably exactly what you think it is: a leaky faucet! But with a clogged drain, the problem could be in the individual drain itself or it could be further down the pipe, so find out if just one drain isn't draining or if all your drains are clogged.

Third, determine if it's a safety issue now or could lead to one. Your family's safety is most important, so if the problem is a safety issue now, or if you think it could lead to one, then you'll probably want to deal with it right away. Remember: just because it may not be a safety issue today doesn't mean it won't be down the road.

Fourth, determine if it's a comfort issue now or in the future. You want your home to be comfortable so if it's not, this should be a priority. Don't forget the comfort of your pets, too! Some comfort issues could become health and safety issues later! For example, if your HVAC system stops working and your house doesn't warm up, that could be a comfort issue today but if your pipes freeze and burst, you've got an incredibly costly problem on your hands that could lead to a damp and moldy basement.

Fifth, determine if your home's value will be impacted. While safety and comfort are often of a higher priority, remember that your home is a significant investment and therefore you may want to make decisions based on the impact it will have on your home's value. For example, upgrading your HVAC system might not be a safety issue if your existing one works just fine, and it might not a comfort issue either if your existing one works just fine, but it could preserve or increase the value of your home by having a more modern high-efficiency HVAC system in your home.

Sixth, understand the true value of hiring an expert. Many homeowners want to find the right service provider to help them. However, it's not always easy to know who can help, and some homeowners end up getting three estimates and choosing the cheapest estimate because they have one convenient number (the price) to compare each service provider against the other. But there are many different service providers and not all of them are the same. In fact, in the upcoming chapters, we'll share with you some of the ways that you can understand the difference between one service provider and another.

Seventh, understand the impact of taking action today. When life gets busy, it's easy to skip over the things that don't seem to be big issues today. However, delaying action can actually increase the price. For example: a leaky faucet today could cost you some money to get repaired today but the overall cost will actually be more if you wait. That's because:

- The cost of water leaking out of your faucets will continue until the faucet is repaired
- The cost of parts rise
- The repair company might be in a busy season when you decide to take action so they may not be able to make it out as soon as you need them

Taking action today is always more cost effective than waiting.

92

Here's The Bottom Line:

If you want to make a wise decision for your family, consider these 7 questions and use them to help you formulate a game-plan to take fast action to fix the problem.

You don't have to spend a long time on these questions but answering them will help you to get the processing moving toward a solution and making your home safer and more comfortable for your family.

ARE YOU MEASURING THE WRONG THING?

Alan and Barb are friends and coworkers, and they both happen to be shopping for a car at the same time. They're both careful shoppers who want to make a smart purchase that will make sense for their families.

After some careful shopping, Alan finds 3 cars that he likes. They all seem similar, so he selects the cheapest car of the three. At the same time, Barb finds 3 cars that she likes. They all seem similar but after some additional research, Barb selects the costliest car of the three.

Alan laughs at Barb and tells her that she got ripped off. After all, he paid a fraction of the price for his car that Barb paid for hers.

The laughter continues… until Alan's tire goes flat. Turns out, his tires were worn out compared to Barb's new tires on her car.

Then Alan's car overheats. Turns out, there was a leak in the radiator. It's not covered under warranty because Alan chose not to spend money on the warranty.

Then, Alan's battery dies and needs to be replaced. Then a sensor goes. Then he needs to replace the headlight. Then his brakes start to squeal.

Alan brings his car back to the dealership and complains that they sold him a lemon. "We don't take returns," says the dealership. So Alan is stuck paying more for his car.

And Barb? She happily drives her car and stops by to pick up Alan to take him to work whenever his car breaks down.

One year later, they both add up what they spent on their car. By now, who do you think has spent more? Barb may have spent more up-front to buy her car but it was Alan who pinched his pennies at the very beginning and thought he was getting the better deal, but is the one who ultimately spent more.

This humorous story is completely true. No, it didn't happen to anyone we know but it happens every single day all across America.

- People buy discount clothes that wear out faster, so they have to spend more to replace those clothes sooner.
- People buy budget services that simply don't fulfill what they need, so they have to make, do or spend more to get more services.
- People buy the lowest-priced gadget and it stops working sooner, so they have to spend more to replace the gadget again and again.
- People buy the cheapest item but it stops working, so they have to spend more to keep it working for them or replace it.

The problem is, many people haven't learned the difference between value and price. That was Alan's problem, and it's a challenge that most people face in the list of challenges above.

Value is the benefit you get from something; price is the amount you pay for something. Both of these are important factors to consider when making a purchase of anything. However, some people focus solely on price and ignore the value they get, and as a result they have to pay more and more in the long-run because the value was not sufficient.

Here's the rule of thumb that you should always keep in mind when purchasing: **Buy for the value it provides. When faced with a choice between offerings of equal value, choose the lowest price.**

That's what Barb did in the story above: she bought for the value the car provided. Her additional research revealed that the cars were not of equal value, so she purchased the car that provided the best value. Alan did the opposite and bought a car without considering the value; he just bought for price.

Here's why this matters to homeowners: Your home is an investment, and if you want to protect it and even potentially increase its value, you need to sometimes invest in your home's maintenance. If you are only making buying decisions based on price, you run the risk of buying something that could actually cost you more in the long-run! However, if you buy based on value then you will save money and frustration.

As home service professionals, we often encounter people who wanted to get 3 or more quotes before they made a decision. There's nothing wrong with being informed or getting quotes. However, we also often got calls from people who said, "I chose to hire someone else because your quote was slightly higher than their quote, but now I've spent money on the other guys and realized that they did a terrible job. Can you come back and fix their mistake?"

If you are comparing estimates and deciding who to hire to work on your home, the most important thing you should be asking yourself is: what is the *value* of this estimate? Don't just look at the price. Consider what the company promises you—that's the value. Then hire the best experts based on the value they bring.

Of course if you have estimates of equal value then it makes sense to choose the lowest price. But rarely will you find estimates of equal value because home service companies are not all the same.

If you had a brain tumor, would you want the best surgeon, who is highly skilled that costs $80,000 for your procedure or would you choose the rookie surgeon who may not have the years of experience behind him for a lesser price?

WHO CAN HELP YOU THE BEST?

Life can get very busy. Between work and soccer practice for the kids, between your social life and your volunteer commitments, between groceries and date night with your partner, there's really not much time for anything else.

That's one reason you love your home—because it is a comfortable oasis away from the busyness of the world.

Unfortunately, when something breaks (or when you're trying to be proactive to care for and maintain our home) it may be hard to know what to do and who to trust to help you.

Should you try to fix something yourself? Should you call your friend who knows a thing or two about plumbing? Should you open the Yellow Pages and just call the first company you see? Should you call the cheapest company? Should you call an expert?

Asking that question ahead of time—before something happens—is a great way to be prepared for when you are ready to take action on your home.

In this chapter, we'll explore each of these questions.

Should You Try To Fix Something Yourself?

Whenever a problem arises with the systems in your home, there are a few things you can do to correct the problem or, at least, to narrow the problem before you need to call someone.

For example, checking that your ducts aren't blocked, resetting the breaker in your circuit panel, plunge the toilet, and even just going over to the neighbor's house to see if they are experiencing the same water discoloration as you are—these are quick, simple, and safe things that you can do right away, and they may solve the problem or help you inform a licensed expert when you schedule an appointment.

Never ever do anything that is unsafe! If you are not sure, don't do it. Instead, call a licensed expert and they may walk you through some other simple options you can do, or send out a licensed expert to help you.

Should You Call Your Friend Who Knows A Thing Or Two About Home Systems?

After working for more than two decades in the home services industry, I can tell you that this happens all the time. For example, Marc doesn't know a lot about plumbing but his friend Bob does. So Marc calls Bob and asks him for help to install a new pipe and faucet for a dishwasher. Bob happily comes over to help and the two of them work together on it.

Seems pretty simple, right? Wrong!

Bob leaves and goes home. A week or two passes. Then Marc wakes up in the middle of the night to a strange noise. The pipe that Bob installed has ruptured and is spewing water all of Marc's expensively renovated basement!

What is marc's recourse? He could try to sue Bob but that's time consuming and costly and who knows if Bob has the money to cover the bill.

Should You Open The Yellow Pages Or Check Online And Just Call The First Company You See?

Although many people do this, there are two challenges to this: First, the Yellow Pages are sorted into alphabetical order, which means that you may overlook a great company that starts with the letter Z because you called a mediocre company that starts with the letter A.

Or, if you choose to call only the companies with big, colorful ads, you're not necessarily calling the best company (you might be but you might not be). Rather, you are calling the company that is willing to spend the most money on ads.

Consider this: would you rather go to a doctor because they will make you healthy? Or because their name started with the letter A and they were willing to out-spend another doctor on an advertisement? Most of us would choose the doctor who would have the best influence on our health!

Should You Call The Cheapest Company?

It pays to be careful with your money. After all, a penny saved is a penny earned, right? You work hard for your money so you should manage what you spend it on.

In addition, many homeowners believe that all home service companies are the same—a plumber is a plumber right? WRONG! (at least in the eyes of the layperson)—so if you get three estimates and one is priced lower than the other, doesn't it make sense to choose the lowest price company?

I would caution you to be careful when comparing estimates and choosing the company that costs the least. ALL ELSE BEING EQUAL, it would make sense to choose the lowest-priced company. If you there were two cars that were EXACTLY the same on a dealership lot and one cost $100 less than the other then it would make perfect sense to choose the cheaper one.

However, the key here is: "ALL ELSE BEING EQUAL" There's something you should know (that you may not be aware of)—most home services companies are NOT equal. Sure, two plumbers or two electricians working for two different home service companies might have the same qualifications, and those two companies might even look similar at a glance, but there are many differences between home service companies, and price should only be one of your deciding factors.

You should also consider factors like:

- How long they've been in business?
- What their client service rating is?
- Whether they are A+ rated with the Better Business Bureau?
- What kind of service they deliver before, during, and after?
- What kind of values the company has?
- Whether the company is an expert in the services you need
- … and more. (See the decision-making checklist in the next chapter.)

You should always choose the BEST company for your home, not just the lowest priced one. Remember: investing in a home service company is an investment into the safety and comfort of your family, and into the value (and resale value) of your home.

Consider these two examples of what happens when you hire the cheapest company:

- Donna got three estimates and chose the cheapest one. The tech showed up but instead of getting to work, he upsold her on a much larger unit than quoted in his original estimate. This "bait-and-switch" tactic allowed the tech to win the project with a lower bid but ultimately charge the higher price.

- Jack got three estimates and chose the one with the cheapest hourly rate. Unfortunately, what Jack didn't realize is that the company with the cheapest hourly rate didn't hire the very best employees. What would have taken any other company 1-2 hours to repair took this cheaper company 3-5 hours to repair, ultimately running up the repair bill much higher (and taking WAY more time) than if Jack had hired one of the seemingly higher-priced companies.

Should You Call An Expert?

Hiring an expert is the best solution.

- An expert gives you the confidence that the problem will be solved. Period.

- An expert gives you confidence that the problem will be solved safely.

- An expert will get the job faster than anyone else (which ultimately saves you money).

- An expert will proactively advise you on other potential problems or opportunities you have in your home to make your home safer and more comfortable.

- An expert will never be pushy or use tricky sales tactics, but will rather advise you of your options and allow you to make the best decision for your family.
- An expert will be fully trained.
- An expert will be licensed.
- An expert will be drug-tested and background-checked.
- An expert will be insured.
- An expert will be professional (you don't have to send the kids out of the room because of something the expert might say!)
- An expert will have clear identification so you know you can safely let them into your house.
- An expert will have all the proper documentation and help to guide you through any permitting requirements.

DECISION-MAKING CHECKLIST

When faced with a decision about your home's safety and comfort systems (including HVAC, electrical, plumbing, drain/sewer, waterproofing, home security and automation, one-day bathroom solutions, water purification, indoor air quality, generators, etc.), you seem to have a lot of choices.

In the last chapter you read about the reasons why you should call a professional company of experts to help you. But when you open the Yellow Pages or go online, it seems like there are a lot of professional companies out there!

In this chapter you'll get a simple, clear decision-making checklist to help you find the very best professional home service expert to help you.

The checklist is simple and works like this:

1. Select 3-5 local companies that you think can help you.
2. Answer these questions for each company.
3. Then choose the one that has the best score.

In just a few minutes you'll have the best answer to your question, "**_Which professional home services expert can help me make my home safer and more comfortable?_**"

You can also download a larger version of this checklist at HomeownersNewswire.com/homeownerschecklist

The Decision-Making Checklist To Help You Find An Expert To Make Your Home Safer And More Comfortable

	Compare our company and two other companies by ranking them based on the factors below.	Company A	Company B	Company C
1.	Are they a branded and recognizable company? (Or have you never heard of them before?)	Y/N	Y/N	Y/N
2.	How long have they been in business?	___	___	___
3.	Who owns the business? (Is it the original owner or a franchiser?)	___	___	___
4.	How many customers have they served?	___	___	___
5.	Are they licensed, bonded, and insured?	Y/N	Y/N	Y/N
6.	Are they recognized with an A+ rating by the Better Business Bureau?	Y/N	Y/N	Y/N
7.	Are they part of a recognizable group that helps and supports homeowners (such as HomeownersNewswire.com)?	Y/N	Y/N	Y/N
8.	What are their hours of operation?	___	___	___

9.	Are their team members cross-trained in all the different systems?	Y/N	Y/N	Y/N
10.	Are they experts in what they do?	Y/N	Y/N	Y/N
11.	Is their team drug-tested and background checked?	Y/N	Y/N	Y/N
12.	Does their team have identification?	Y/N	Y/N	Y/N
13.	Does their team use floormats and boot protectors?	Y/N	Y/N	Y/N
14.	Do they have testimonials from other satisfied homeowners (whether on their website or on social media)?	Y/N	Y/N	Y/N
	Which company has the best results? *(See scoring instructions below)*	—	—	—

Scoring instructions:

For Y/N questions: Y = 3 points; N = 0 points

For all other questions: award 3 points to the best answer, 2 points to the middle answer, and 1 point to the worst answer. (Or zero points if you don't know the answer).

For example: Company A served 140,000 customers, Company B served 60,000 customers, and Company C didn't reveal how many customers they served.

8.	How many customers have they served?	140K	60K	???

Then you would give 3 points to Company A, 2 points to Company B, and 0 points to Company C.

Now simply add up the points for each one and place that number at the bottom of the chart, like this:

	Which company has the best results? *(See scoring instructions below)*	43	28	10

The higher number, the better! Now you have a simple, at-a-glance way to see which company can help you make your home safer and more comfortable for your family.

HERE'S THE SURPRISING THING NO ONE TELLS YOU (AND IT CAN SAVE YOU A LOT OF HASSLE!)

When our experts show up at customers' homes because something broke down, one of the things we often hear is, "I didn't realize this was not working properly until it broke."

You lead a busy life and, chances are, you probably don't spend a lot of time thinking about how your HVAC, plumbing or electrical systems are working… Until they stop working!

There's nothing wrong with not paying a lot of attention to these systems! You have a lot to think about and, for the most part, these systems work just fine.

You might live your busy life with the confidence you've placed in these home systems and suddenly they don't quite function the way you want them to!

When they stop working the way you want them to, that's when the hassle starts. That's when you go to the internet to search for what's wrong, or you call up a friend to ask them for a quick over-the-phone assessment of what's wrong.

Problem is, that investigation is hard to do when you yourself aren't an expert in the system and you're just trying to search the internet or explain to a friend what the problem is. And it's worse if it's an emergency, such as if there is water rushing into your basement and you don't know why or where it's coming from—the internet or that friend won't be able to help you very much.

It's like having an extremely sore elbow but instead of going to the doctor, you search online—there are many reasons for that sore elbow and it really needs an expert to assess the situation.

Fortunately, there's a simple solution to solve this challenge. By doing this one simple solution;

- You'll save yourself a lot of money by avoiding mistakes and wrong decisions.

- You'll save yourself even more money by proactively addressing problems before they become large, costly problems.

- You'll save yourself a lot of time because you can make faster decisions (and they won't be rushed).

- You'll eliminate the hassle because you can think through a solution with all the information.

- You'll make your home safer and more comfortable… and keep it that way.

The secret is: find a trusted expert who can help you with all of your home's systems and services, and then build a relationship with them to proactively care for your home.

Maybe that sounds weird to you because, in the past, you have only ever called a home service company when you needed something—such as when a pipe burst or when you needed to upgrade your water heater or when your HVAC system was making a funny noise.

But here's the secret that some people know and it saves them so much time, money, and stress: your home service expert is a lot like your mechanic or doctor. Some people just go to a mechanic or doctor when something is wrong. But smart people go for regular check-ups regularly even when nothing seems wrong.

- When the expert sees things running normally, and becomes familiar with your home and its systems, that provides a "knowledge baseline" just like a mechanic might need to know about how your car performs in the best of conditions or like what your doctor might need to know about how your body functions when you are well.

- The expert has tools and strategies that can detect potential problems before they become bigger, catastrophic, costlier problems, to help you fix things while they are still minor.

- The expert can make proactive suggestions about ways to increase the safety and comfort of your family based on what they know about your family.

This is only possible when you build a relationship with a home services expert; when they come to your house and see things working normally; when you can sit down with them and discuss what your home is like and what goals you have for the safety and comfort of your family. (Conversely, this can't happen if you only ever call the first available home service company to come right away because your water heater just burst all over your basement.

Just like your doctor, have an expert come in and do a check-up on your home, and schedule these check-ups regularly. You will be far more proactive in enhancing the safety and comfort of your home!

We can't recommend this strongly enough! If you only take one single action after reading: **find a trusted home services company and have them send an expert to your home to do a home services check-up. Then, schedule that check-up to occur at least every 6 months for as long as you own a home.**

Build a relationship with that company by using one company and by proactively having their experts visit your home from time to time to perform a check-up.

Imagine the peace of mind you'll feel when you see this truck pull in your driveway...

Our team is ready to serve you. We want to make your home safe and comfortable for your family and we'll do everything we can to WOW you with our service.

Do you know a friend, relative, neighbor, or coworker that we can WOW with our service too? Next time you hear someone complaining at work about a leaky faucet, or worrying about the quality of water that their family is drinking, tell them to call us.

ABOUT THE AUTHOR

Steve Addario was born and raised in Massachusetts. He started his career as an plumber and then partnered with his brother Joseph Addario to build Addario's Services, the #1 rated home service company in Massachusetts, providing electrical, plumbing, HVAC, drain cleaning, and more, to more than 30,000 customers.

Steve is a committed leader in the community, participating in local service organizations for the purpose of improving his community.

You might have seen Steve on ABC, CBS, NBC, Fox, or read articles about him or by him in Contractor Magazine, and more.

Steve is a martial arts practitioner. He is married to Alison and has 4 children, 2 dogs, 2 guinea pigs, and chickens.

GET IN TOUCH WITH US

1-877-ADDARIOS
2 3 3-2 7 4 6

www.addarios.com

dispatch@addarios.com

Our call center is open 24/7 and is staffed by local experts who can help you right away.

VISIT OUR WEBSITE (AND GET $2,500 IN MONEY-SAVING COUPONS!)

Visit and bookmark our website for even more tips and ideas to help you enjoy a safer and more comfortable home for your family.

While you're there, enter your email address for immediate access to $2,500 in money-saving coupons for many of the services you need around your home.

www.addarios.com

http://www.addarios.com/coupons/

Made in the USA
Middletown, DE
09 August 2020